THE ~~A~~
of
RAPID RE~~A~~

A book for
people who want to read
faster and more accurately

BY
WALTER B. PITKIN

PUBLISHERS *Grosset & Dunlap* NEW YORK

ACKNOWLEDGMENTS

I wish to acknowledge with thanks the privilege of reprinting, for use in exercises, several articles and news items from *The New York Times;* from the publications of the McGraw-Hill Book Company, Inc.; from "The New Reformation," by Michael Pupin, published by Charles Scribner's Sons; and from "The Twilight of the American Mind," by Walter B. Pitkin, published by Simon and Schuster. Each reprint is individually accredited.

I particularly wish to thank Professor E. L. Thorndike and the Bureau of Publications of Teachers College for permission to use some parts of the Thorndike word list as vocabulary exercises.

THE AUTHOR.

HOW TO READ THIS BOOK

This book has three divisions of instructive reading matter. They are the Introduction, Part I, and Part II.

Please Read These Three Straight Through as You Would Read a Magazine Article. Do Not Stop to Analyze Anything. Do Not Stop to Perform Any Exercises. First Form a General Impression of the Whole Subject.

Then Go Back and Read Intensively. Directly after This Perform at Least a Few of the Exercises.

When you begin reading this book, turn to the Progress Chart in Part VI and start making a record of your reading speed.

WARNING ABOUT THE EXERCISES

The value of the exercises in this book depends largely on your being unfamiliar with their content when you try them.

Do not turn through the book and read the text of any exercise.

Omit every exercise which you may have accidentally read in advance.

CONTENTS

PART IV

PART V

PART VI

THE ART OF RAPID READING

THE ART OF RAPID READING

INTRODUCTION

The art of communication has three grand divisions. The first involves mastery of the *subject*. The second involves mastery of its *presentation*, which is usually in written form. The third involves mastery of its *reception*, which is listening to a spoken presentation and reading of a written presentation.

Our schools and colleges originally devoted themselves chiefly to teaching subjects. Many years ago business and professional men began to discover that they were unable to present the subjects they knew in an effective form. Then began the education of writers. Courses in Business English multiplied. Scientific bodies and technical corporations undertook to instruct their staffs in the art of speaking and writing. Today, in the United States at least, it is fair to say that we have advanced far in making practical writers of engineers, executives, and editors and reporters of trade and technical journals. No country in the world produces nearly so much as ours in the way of clearly written reports, articles, and textbooks dealing with the affairs of business, industry, and the techniques.

But this very success brings to light our deficiencies in the third and last of the arts of communication. We have plenty of people who know their subjects. We have an astonishing number of excellent writers among those who know their subjects. And they are writing far more

1

than their public can read.   Can we not train this public
to keep up in its reading?

I am sure that we can—at least to a very considerable
degree.

This book is strictly for the busy adult who is dissatisfied
with the amount of reading he does in the course of a year.
It will be of little or no value to school children.   Eminent
specialists have written excellent books for them.   Their
problems are very different from those with which we are
going to wrestle here.   So far as I know, nobody has
given the poor adult a serious thought.

And yet all of the world's important reading is done
by this same poor adult.   The fate of nations hangs on
what he reads.   So does the trend in the stock markets.
So does the march of industry and business.   So does the
progress of education and every larger aspect of social
welfare.   Abolish reading matter.   Abolish readers.   And
what have you left?   A world of talkers.   How much
business could they do, as compared with the readers who
also talk?

Surely not one-tenth as much.   Or, if as much as that
in bulk, then surely of inferior quality.   For men misunder-
stand one another far more in conversation than in the
printed word.   Why so?   Because a word once spoken
has vanished; and, unless you have correctly grasped
its relation to all else that is being said, you become
confused.

Did you ever suffer from having your talk reported?
Did you ever give an address of which you failed to
prepare a summary for the newspapers?   Then you know
what I mean.   We complain bitterly of the blunders
the reporters commit when digesting our talk.   But we
fail to consider that everybody tends to misinterpret
what we say, and mainly because the ear does not retain
large masses of speech in a form that can be reviewed later

as easily as you review a printed page. When you fail to grasp a printed statement, you run your eye back and look the words over afresh. That can't be done with sounds.

So, if you wish to *persuade* a man quickly, talk to him; for your personality will impress him more intensely than the precise content of your remarks. But if you wish to *inform* a man, give him your ideas to study with care, in some permanent form.

Talk is the salesman's proper medium. But print is the best one for the buyer, for the manager, and for the junior executive. Talk excites and moves to action. But the printed word conveys truth, instructs, and commands. Salesmen always dislike doing business through the printed word (and this includes the typed letter, of course). Naturally! And when salesmen are promoted into executive posts where their primary duty is not selling but managing men and affairs, they tend to carry over this prejudice. They incline to do everything by conversation and harangue. And, without realizing it, they cramp their style badly. Talk, used where print serves better, is a contagious disease in American business.

In 1917, I dropped in on a business man who was then engaged in large-scale international administration and listened to the growls of many subordinates over a strict order which he had issued. The order assumed the visible form of a card propped up on everybody's desk, in all too plain sight. It read: "*Verbal Orders Do Not Go Here.*"

I heard how dreadfully this rule was slowing down work and causing profound spiritual unrest. And yet—and yet! The boss managed to transact several billion dollars of business under this anti-talk law. His name, by the way, was Herbert Hoover; and he was feeding the world.

Talk has two other weaknesses. It must be uttered in the presence of your audience, and its rate of delivery is between one-quarter and one-third that of reading matter. This allows, of course, for the inevitable breaks, silences, minor interruptions, hemming and hawing, and sundry oratorical effects which always creep into sustained conversation and speeches. Business men seldom average better than 80 words a minute in their talk; but, if properly drilled, they can easily read between 200 and 300 words of serious matter per minute.

In business dealings, all of us tend to talk too much and read too little. This cannot be charged wholly against the salesman's habits and preferences. It is surely caused in no small measure by imperfect early training in school. I am forced to this conclusion by many personal observations. I have seen many distinguished business executives who have graduated from good colleges without attaining the speed or the accuracy in reading which we should expect of a high-school boy. Let me cite a case or two. The matter is important enough to be thus emphasized.

A magazine once published a brief and clearly organized summary of a survey I made of openings in various professional fields. The article, as I recall, did not run above 1,500 words. Many business men commented on it variously; among them, a high official in one of our finest manufacturing corporations. He enumerated, in his criticism of my argument, six statements which he attributed to me. All of these he found in the article. But, oddly enough, not one of them appeared there, nor anywhere else. He had read the text so inaccurately that he completely reversed its meaning. Result? He attacked me for holding views which I myself had attacked, and he championed every view I held!

Here is a worse one. Some years ago I wrote a report of trade conditions for a certain concern. It was, to be sure, somewhat technical and not easy reading; but it was made as clear as the subject permitted. And it was designed to be read only by a few people who were familiar with the subject. When the president of the company studied it, he wrote a series of comments on it which revealed that he had quite missed the main points. No other reader missed them. I asked him, therefore, to point out where he had found basis for his interpretations. He waded laboriously through the pages, wasted two or three hours of his time and mine, and finally admitted that he must have read too fast. Truth was he had read poorly.

Lest you conclude that I am picking meanly on the business man, I close this sad tale with the worst case of all, which reveals that workers in other fields are quite as poor readers. Last year I checked up on the accuracy with which the reviewers of some important books had stated the facts about the contents of the books. Matters of opinion were ignored; only such things as were indisputable were counted. It appeared that about half of the book reviews were childishly inaccurate. And yet here we have to do with people who presumably are fast and accurate readers. Why otherwise should they be reviewing books?

So, you see, we have a large job on our hands! We must help most adults make up for the deficiencies in their early training.

THE THREE ARTS OF READING

There are three distinct arts of reading. Each art has its own purpose. Each deals with more or less different material. And each develops quite distinct methods. Unfortunately, teachers have not made this clear to learners; hence much bad reading.

The three purposes determine the three arts. For they first of all determine both the material to be read and the way in which it is to be read. So we must look at them first of all.

When we are very young, we first read in order to learn things; and, as we grow up, some of us lose interest in self-development, while others of us pursue our favorite studies ever more intensively.

Early in life most of us also read for the fun of it. Story books open the door to delightful realms of fancy. We escape the matter-of-fact world and roam whither the creative imagination of novelists and dramatists leads us. As the world of bread and butter makes sterner demands upon our time and efforts, most of us have to restrict such pleasure reading considerably. Before the thirtieth year, most men and women have reduced it to a mere fraction of what it was during their 'teens. But, as leisure becomes more general, pleasure reading claims more time.

Finally, most of us develop an interest in reading for current information. To some extent, this overlaps with the first purpose of reading for self-improvement. But it is in the main a distinct enterprise. We scan the daily newspaper merely to see what's going on in the big world and in our neighborhood. We want to know whether our railroad stock has gone up or down since yesterday. We wonder how our college football team came out in its big game with its ancient rival. And did Mrs. Murphy sail for Paris with her daughter, or are they going to Palm Beach for the winter?

Keeping in touch with events that concern us—that is the third purpose of reading. And, in modern America, it has become a huge task. So many things are happening! So many people are busily making them happen! Furthermore, news in one's field of business now flows, a mighty stream. There is more going on in the realm of the automobile trade than was happening in all Europe a generation ago. Events in the women's wear trade are numerous enough and important enough to be reported in a special daily newspaper. So with Wall Street events. And virtually every industry in America has its own weeklies or monthlies whose chief aim is to give news of special interest.

Now it is a well-known fact that each day has only twenty-four hours, and day follows day in relentless procession. The reader must move with the calendar, or else fall behind in his grasp of events. The sales manager who fails to survey the morning's report of affairs that touch his field will soon make a ghastly mistake. The investor who is contemplating purchase of copper stocks becomes a mere gambler if he ignores the latest news about the copper industry and every trade that affects it. Thus throughout the entire range of business, finance, politics, and manufacturing.

Here, then, we see the necessity of a third art of reading. Here we come upon material and problems which differ profoundly from those we encounter when we read merely to educate ourselves or for personal delight. In studying cultural subjects, we master everything as we go. We analyze, we make notes perhaps, we stop to ponder over the whole range of facts from time to time. Our speed is set almost wholly by the intricacy and strangeness of the subject matter and by our wish to master it through and through. When, on the other hand, we read for sheer pleasure, we set our own pace. Whatever speed gives us the most pleasure is the right speed. And nobody can lay down rules for us here. Some of us enjoy novels best when we skim them lightly, while others choose to linger over colorful phrases and to go lost in revery suggested by the tale. Some of us must read the book straight through at a sitting, while others like to sip at it at intervals.

How different the procedure when we read in order to keep in touch with affairs in our profession, our art, our trade, or our business! Here Father Time sets the pace, and Competition is the referee. We must cover ground or lose out. We must pick and choose material that specially touches our practical interests and fortunes. We dare not let our private taste and pleasure rule us. Nor can we be studious and thorough in the manner of the cultural reader. Hence, we must work out a third art of reading. And this is the subject of the book now in your hands.

Whoever reads it, thinking it a guide in school work or in pleasure reading, will make a sorry mess of it. Here and there he will find something that serves well in the first and second arts. But the technique as a whole does not.

WHAT WILL YOU GAIN?

Now let us see what you stand to gain by pursuing the exercises that follow in this book. Naturally, I can offer only a general answer applicable to most readers. Some will far exceed my estimate, while a few will fall far below it.

First of all, how long must you work at them in order to get useful results? Tests on adults made at the University of Chicago, Columbia, and elsewhere show that fairly persistent self-drill for 30 or 60 days will yield marked improvement in one's reading, both as to speed and as to comprehension.

Three to four months of drill will bring you to the peak of improvement, as a rule. What does this mean as to your velocity and grasp?

Here are a few simple comparisons. Apply them to your own case and find your own answer. Obviously, we cannot set up a universal standard to which all men must conform; for the material you have to read in your business differs considerably from the material I must read, and so, too, do circumstances differ under which we read.

Here are four fairly typical levels of reading. I omit skimming, as it falls in a class by itself.

Light Reading.

Ordinary newspaper items and the simpler varieties of fiction are usually read at the rate of five or six words per second. This speed can be maintained for an hour or two, without strain.

Suppose you spend two hours daily throughout the year on such light reading. Your annual coverage would then amount to 13,000,000 words more or less (5 words per second equals 18,000 words per hour or 1,080,000 per month of two hours daily reading).

This Would Equal 130 Books of 100,000 Words Each.

Average Reading.

The longer newspaper articles on serious subjects and most ordinary news articles in business and trade papers in your own special fields can be read at four words a second, up to a total of two hours daily.

If you devote two hours daily to such reading matter, you can cover in a year between 10,000,000 and 10,500,000 words (4 words per second equal 14,400 per hour).

This Would Equal 100 Books of 105,000 Words Each.

Solid Reading.

Technical discussions of fairly difficult matters more or less unfamiliar to you will slow your speed down to 3 words per second. At this rate your annual coverage would run around 7,000,000 or 8,000,000 words, which would equal some 70 or 80 volumes of standard size.

Heavy Reading.

Technical dicussions of subjects almost wholly new to you and important enough to require thorough understanding of them must be studied, rather than read. Here you will be doing well if you average 6,000 words per hour. And it is unlikely that you will be able to devote two hours daily to such intensive perusal throughout the year. Suppose, however, that you do this. Then you ought to cover between 4,000,000 and 4,500,000 words annually; or the equivalent of 40 to 50 books of standard length.

Nobody spends all his time on any one of these four reading levels. We have to spread our efforts over all in some combination. Suppose that you were to divide your daily time in the following more or less typical manner:

	Minutes
To light reading, including some newspaper skimming	15
To average reading	45
To solid reading	30
To heavy reading (study)	30

On this basis you would read, in the course of one year:

Of light reading	1,600,000 words, or 16 books of standard length.
Of average reading	3,900,000 words, or 39 books of standard length.
Of solid reading	2,000,000 words, or 20 books of standard length.
Of heavy reading	1,000,000 words, or 10 books of standard length.

On a gross average, this would mean that you would finish the equivalent of a book every four and one-half days, year in, year out!

Perhaps you can find only one hour daily for reading. Even so, see what you can accomplish! On this modest basis you can read:

8 books of the light type.

17 books of average difficulty.

10 books of solid reading.

5 books requiring close study.

Or a total of 40 books a year.

Now, Virtually Every American Business Man Whose Eyes are Moderately Good Can Equal This Rate. Not One in a Thousand is Unable to Find Seven Hours Weekly for Reading.

Suppose that three-quarters of all your average and solid reading matter were in business magazines and trade or technical journals. And suppose that you were spending, all told, only one hour daily on all kinds of reading, as above described. How much ground would you be covering in a year in such periodicals alone?

About 3,750,000 words. Or 750 articles of 5,000 words each. Suppose you concentrated on magazines; you would be reading 10 such articles monthly in six periodicals throughout the year.

All These Estimates Are Based on the Average Speed of Reading by Adults Who Have Not Specially Trained Themselves to Cover Ground Fast and Thoroughly.

It has been demonstrated that fairly intelligent people can improve their speed and comprehension fully 50 per cent above the rates I have been using in these hypothetical cases.

Were You to Make the Effort, You Could Probably Cover, in One Hour Daily throughout the Year:

12 books of the light type,

25 books of average difficulty,

15 books of solid reading, and

8 books requiring close study.

Or a total of 60 books yearly. Better than a book a week!

A man will gladly sweat two hours a day for years, in order to excel at tennis. And, having achieved this excellence, all he can do is to beat his friends in the innocent art of swatting a rubber ball over a net.

Suppose he spent half as much energy mastering the much harder game of language. What would he have to show for his efforts afterward? Well, he would be able to keep in touch with world affairs far faster and more accurately than most other people. He would almost certainly have mastered some subject that interested him; for, in the course of sustained and intensive reading, normally he would have been reading serious books and magazines whose content interested him. Finally, it would be odd if incidentally he had not improved his own conversational abilities. And this would improve him as a social creature.

I do not deem it an exaggeration to say that "reading maketh a full man" in business quite as much as in culture; or that a man who can and does read along serious lines related to his life work in the volume we have just been indicating must acquire immense advantages, in the long run, over his rivals who are less well read. After all, success depends essentially upon two things, *knowing* the markets and *dealing* in the markets. And most knowledge comes through the printed word.

Time spent on these reading exercises ought to aid one's business quite as much as time spent on designing more efficient machines in the factory. For man's mind is the most marvelous of all machines. To improve it is to improve all the things it moves and creates.

This is not an inspirational book. It is a sweat shop. You, gentle reader, are to do all the work, while I sit back and sing out "One-two! One-two!" like those Kings of Calisthenics who warble at you every morning over the radio when you tune in on your bedside exercises.

You want to improve your reading. Very well! You must read and read and read. All I shall do is to give you sundry useful tips as to your procedure.

For every word I write here, you will have to read a thousand or more.

Does the book seem very short? Well, think it over after you have finished all the exercises! If you take our instructions in the proper spirit, the book will keep you on the jump for the remainder of your life. For one of its most earnest contentions is that, once you have attained a new high level of ability, you will have to go on using this ability if you wish to possess it.

All skill depends on exercise. Continued skill depends on continued exercise. Paderweski said something on this which deserves to be quoted again.

> If I go one day without practising at the piano, I notice it in my playing. If I go two days, my friends notice it. If I go three days, the audience notices it.

You cannot be a fast and efficient reader unless you read and read and read. Practice makes perfect. And perfection, once attained, is retained only through continued practice. So I am now trying not only to improve your reading but to make of you a chronic and voluminous reader.

ON THE RELATIVE IMPORTANCE OF THINGS

You will never become a skilful reader unless you first cultivate a fairly keen sense of the *relative importance of things*. And this, alas, is something I cannot teach you in any wee volume like this one. It is, as a matter of fact, the quintessence of genuine education and culture.

I know a jolly professor of philosophy who reads his Sunday newspaper straight through, line by line, skipping only some of the advertisements.   Usually he finishes the job around Tuesday evening.   Now a metaphysician may read thus, for to him all things are of almost equal importance. But nobody else dares to do so.   We must pick and choose. We must budget our interests, as well as our time and our money.   Otherwise we accomplish nothing.

The first stage in reading is to select what we ought to read and to discard everything else.   To learn what is worth our while is a large part of the Art of Life.   And here I must assume that you, as adults in a busy world, have mastered this task.   What you may not have mastered as yet is the special application of your wants and needs to the printed page; that is, to the actual job of running your eye along the lines of type and picking out the useful.

To make your eye the servant of your will is the particular aim of the present exercise in reading.   You must come to the task with a clear will.   Otherwise you will profit little.

When you pick up a newspaper or a magazine, you ought to glance through it in much the same spirit as you look over the immense display on large newsstands.   Here you see printed matter about aviation, physical culture, engineering, retail merchandising, golf, tennis, interior decoration, and heaven knows what not.   Does it ever occur to you to buy all these periodicals?   Not if you are sane.   You select from the mass a few which have some special interest to you.

So with the articles inside of any one of them.   You must carry your selecting through to a finish here.   In the first instance, you buy selectively in order to save your money.   In the second instance, you ought to read selectively in order to save your time.

Time is far more important than money.   Time is life. In the career of any well-regulated human being, one hour ought to be worth a good many dollars. Whenever you dawdle over printed words which neither enlighten nor amuse you, you are partly committing suicide.

Many people are dead from the ears up because they are dying by the hour. And when you die, you die from the top down.

HOW TO READ FOR RELATIVE IMPORTANCES

The first law of skilful reading is merely an application of the Law of Relative Importance. You must perceive, first of all, the total offerings of the printed matter; then you must appraise these. Get the larger picture first; see the whole exhibit, then go to details.

Read Wholes, Not Parts. Read Sentences, Not Words.

Read for the Broadest Meanings First, Then for Details Later if Necessary.

This is no fad. It is the sound teaching of psychology. We all learn things most rapidly and most thoroughly when we tackle them in their entirety.

If you wish to learn to play the piano, you progress best in the long run by playing the pieces as written. You waste time and probably confuse yourself if you plunge through one-finger exercises, attempting to learn the parts of the composition separately.

Children learn to talk in this same manner. They seldom learn words first. They talk sentences, even though the latter may not conform to adult grammar and style.

The Normal Human Being First Experiences Things in Masses. Later He Analyzes Them into Their Parts.

Reading is a Mode of Learning. It Should, Therefore, Follow The Laws of Learning. And This is the First of Those Laws.

Of the two wrong ways to read, namely reading word by word and skimming, the latter is by far the better. It is closer to nature.

Beware of taking elaborate notes *while you read*. There is no less efficient habit.

Read first, then reflect; and, if you do not retain clearly the gist of what you have read, go back over the material and take notes on things you have failed to remember.

This rule applies to such things as statistics and formulas. When you run across valuable material of this sort, it is best not to stop reading for the sake of copying it. Make a mark in the book or magazine and come back to it after you have finished reading. Then copy.

Why do thus? Because here as everywhere else, *Do One Thing at a Time and Do That Well*. Note taking is not reading. Comprehending the chief meanings is not the same as making a permanent record of some detail.

Much time is lost, and even more content is blurred, by the misguided attempt to alternate between reading and notes.

Read straight ahead. Do not stop unless you lose the main line of thought. Never mind the obscurity of details.

GRASPING THE ESSENTIALS

In many instances, you need to gather only the main fact from what you read. The art of finding this differs considerably from the art of perceiving masses of detail.

If all authors wrote well, it would be an easy art to teach. For then you would find the central thought clearly stated in the opening lines of the article. You would also find the major subdivisions indicated in a clear visual form throughout the text.

Fortunately, most of our scientific and technical journals are approaching this ideal—though some have still a long mile to travel. They adapt newspaper technique to their own special purposes.

A newspaper will outline a news item in three or four stages of completeness. The top headline will indicate the *main event* in the briefest possible phrase. The lower headlines will amplify this within 40 or 50 words. Then the lead paragraph will carry the story one degree further along. After that will come all the lesser details.

The technical and scientific journal will do likewise, but in a more formal fashion. Here is a typical arrangement.

1. The subject of the paper:
   Usually stated in a short paragraph.
2. Details.
3. Summary of facts.
4. Conclusions reached from facts.
5. Bibliography, if any.

One of the surest ways for you to improve your reading is to do what you can by way of persuading editors and book publishers to cast important material into some such readily comprehended form. This will save you hours in the course of every month. And it may even add more to your effective span of life than all the golf and motoring you do.

USE THE TABLE OF CONTENTS AND THE PREFACE

You will usually save much time and come with greater ease to the essentials of a book, if you make it a practice to study its table of contents and preface with some care. Unfortunately some authors of serious books do not take their table of contents seriously enough. They do not aid their readers as they should in getting a bird's-eye view at the outset.

Naturally you need make such a survey only when you are plunging into the entire book. When reading for a special topic, whose relation to the larger subject you know in advance, this method is needless.

PART I

THE CAUSES OF POOR READING

We vary in our speed of reading to an astonishing degree.

The vice-president of a large textile company says, "It takes me a couple of weeks to read a book such as my boy of fourteen reads in an evening. Probably he could tell you the gist of it as well as I could, too." Contrast to him a woman I know who thinks nothing of reading three, four, or even five fat books in the course of a day, all of which she retains with considerable accuracy.

Even more widely do we vary in our speed of skimming. Every experienced newspaper editor races over hundreds of thousands of words every week and manages to hold in his memory quite enough to give him his bearings about a thousand and one news items for as long as these are of value to him in his business.

Where do you fall between these extremes? If near to this lady, my little book cannot be of any use to you. If, on the other hand, you find it hard to read, let us say, 65 to 75 pages of a fairly serious non-fiction book in about two hours, these exercises will almost certainly help you.

If they do nothing more, they will surely assist you in discovering the causes of your own slow or unsure reading. The exercises are planned to test each of the chief factors in reading singly. Some of these factors are beyond bettering through drill. For example, defective eyesight. Most of them fortunately may be improved. Your problem is to ascertain which call for such treatment.

A simple outline may clear matters here. Suppose that at this very moment you pick up a book and say: "I must read Chapter VII in this work at once." What factors play in upon your act and the reading which ensues? They group as follows:

1. The *interests* that lead you to read the book.

2. The *habits* of body and mind that you use in the act of reading.

3. The *momentary conditions* under which your interests and habits of reading operate. These momentary conditions fall into three important rough classes:

    a. Conditions of your *surroundings*,

    b. Conditions of your *physique*, and

    c. Conditions of your *mind*.

1. YOUR INTERESTS IN READING

There are scores of possible interests, hundreds of habits, and an all but infinite variety of momentary conditions. Nothing short of minute self-analysis will reveal to you the source of your own short-comings as a reader. Look first at the interests that may be at work in moving you to select the particular chapter and book for reading now. Later we shall show how you may adjust your methods to your actual interests.

Your primary interests in reading that chapter of that book at this moment may be nothing more than self-protection. Your general sales manager may have called a conference for this afternoon and may have announced that everybody who attends it ought to check through the market statistics given in that particular passage. To save your face, you are going to glance at the pages; for it will be humiliating to be called upon to express an opinion on them and to admit lack of knowledge. Reading therefore is merely a means to the end of standing in well with your sales manager.

Or you may read in order to refute the author, who has attacked some of your pet methods of managing men.

Or you may read solely to check up on a calculation you made yesterday which involved some of the reported statistics. Or you may read to find confirmation of one of your pet theories. Or you may read because, not knowing the statistics, you need them in your business and decide to master them.

Now, *Your Interest in Reading Ought to Determine the Way You Read.* It is wasteful, therefore foolish, to pursue one and only one reading method for all kinds of matter and all interests. Your school teachers never taught you this. They merely taught you to read and usually the interest they forced upon you was that of reading in order to pass a school examination on what you read. This forced you to cram on all the petty details of the text.

Is it any wonder that so many young people developed a dislike of literature? Or that they failed to become expert readers? America, I grieve to say, is full of pedants who drill the young to read the wonderful pages of Thackeray, Kipling, and Balzac as if these were population statistics compiled by the Census Bureau, and as if the young were reading them in the capacity of proofreaders and statisticians. They must be able to name all the characters, all the big scenes, the themes, plots, and what not. Otherwise they fail in the so-called Literature Course and are set down as poor students!

If you read novels slowly and have a vague feeling of hard work, it is more than likely that you are now paying the penalty of having been taught to read the classics by some educated imbecile who never understood that the one proper interest in reading Thackery, Kipling, and Balzac is intellectual and emotional entertainment. The manner of reading them must fit this interest; in short, you must read in an entertaining manner. And the author must first write in an entertaining manner.

Pleasure Reading and Serious Reading

We are here concerned solely with improving your serious reading. Though we shall not discuss the lighter varieties of pleasure reading, it is not amiss to warn you that you must not expect, in reading your engineers' reports and trade journals, to approach the speed at which you race through the novels of Zane Grey and the pages of the *Saturday Evening Post.*

Short stories, novels, and popular magazine articles are written for relaxation. They are cast into the easiest of all forms for reading. As far as possible they are told in dramatic narrative and in episodes. The words they use are usually familiar and colorful. The characters and situations described have an elemental human interest.

Even poorly educated readers can read such material at the rate of 12,000 words per hour. This, by the way, is the average velocity indicated for the short articles and stories published by *Liberty,* which, as you know, used to announce at the opening of each the reading time required. A well-educated reader who has drilled himself thoroughly can, with no effort whatsoever, read this sort of matter at the rate of 18,000 or 20,000 words per hour. And a seasoned manuscript editor will flash through 25,000 words per hour.

The material a business or professional man has to read, however, rarely can be cast into such a simple mould. Complex affairs have to be reported and analyzed. Technical language must be used. And easy reading must always be sacrificed for the sake of accuracy.

The reader's attitude increases the difference. He picks up a novel in the spirit of adventure and a good time. He will not be bored. Nor will he toil. Woe to the fiction that doesn't please him! He lays it aside and finds something better suited to his mood.

That free and easy manner doesn't go, though, when he enters his office keyed up to the morning's work. How changed his purpose! How much firmer the will to achieve! No complaint over difficulties! No shirking of details! Business is business! And that tells the whole story.

Later I shall talk about the art of skimming. Then you will learn, in some detail, that *Each Interest Moving You to Read Causes You to Select and to Stress Certain Features of the Reading Matter. And for Many Legitimate Interests the Best of All Methods is to Skim the Text Very Lightly but with a Sure Feel for Whatever Happens to Be Relevant to Your Interest. This Art of Skimming is the Highest and Finest of All the Arts of Reading. Pedants Imagine It is the Opposite. But Professional Workers Who Do Much Reading Know that Intelligent Skimming is Hard and Immensely Profitable.*

Just now I am suggesting only that part of your difficulty in fast, sure reading may be due to a maladjustment between your interests and your manner of reading. You may be interested in nothing beyond one specific fact in the chapter book; yet you may pore over every word as if you had to thresh all the chaff for the sake of one kernel of wheat. Again, your interest may be to ascertain the underlying argument of the author; but you center your attention erroneously upon many of his specific facts which do not belong to that argument at all. Or, what is perhaps more probable, you read only a general interest in the subject at hand, hence grope around as you read in search of a more definite interest.

What is the cure for such a maladjustment? Simply a clear understanding of the manner of reading which best fits your interest in reading the particular page. As you go on in these exercises you will pick up this trick. Meanwhile ask yourself quite seriously, as you open a magazine or book: "Just why am I going to read now? Just what do I want to get out of it?"

Also, please take me quite seriously when I say that for some interests it is quite enough to read the table of contents of a book, for other interests it is better to read the index and follow up two or three references in it, while for still others it is best to read the summary chapter at the end of the volume. Sometimes you ought to skim as lightly as a summer swallow. Sometimes you ought to swallow everything in sight.

Your Aim Determines Your Method.

The worst of all possible ways to read is in the passive manner. You will get little or nothing from the printed page if you bring to it nothing but your eye. You will get the most from it if you approach it with some definite interest and purpose. Strange as it may sound, it is none the less literally true that a man will gain a great deal more than a passive reader can if he approaches the page with a trivial or silly purpose. To say to yourself as you open the book, "Well, I wonder how many fool remarks this idiot will foist on me" is vastly more useful than to say or think nothing.

2. YOUR HABITS

Habits of body count no less than habits of mind in reading. Posture and activity must be carefully analyzed.

A. POSTURE

For convenience, rather than as a matter of logic, I shall here class together three kinds of position:

1. The actual bodily position.
2. This position relative to the printed page.
3. This position relative to the illumination.

1. Posture, in the narrower sense, is the body's own position; that is, the position of its members relative to one another. So far as reading is concerned, posture is

important in so far as it affects (*a*) The circulation of your blood, and (*b*) The tension of your muscles.

Any posture that disturbs blood circulation is bad. So is any posture that causes any muscles to become tense.

Fig. 1.—Bad position of body. The back is curved, and the head is dropped. Circulation of the blood is disturbed. The eyes fatigue rapidly and reading becomes drudgery in short order. Neither speed nor high comprehension can be maintained.

The two commonest bad postures are bending low over the printed page, and lying flat and looking up at the printed page.

These are by no means equally bad for all persons. Some of us find that we read fairly well while lying flat, at least for a little while; and we get a special satisfaction from it because in this position we relax those muscles which have been tense in the course of the day's work. People who are on their feet all day often find the recumbent position excellent for reading. Sedentary workers are less likely to. In any case, however, check up on yourself.

FIG. 2.—Body position of doubtful value. People differ considerably in their ability to read while lying down. Some of us are deceived into thinking that we read well thus, when as a matter of fact, we are simply comfortable in our bones and muscles. As a relief from standing or sitting all day long, lying down is excellent. And for some readers it is a fairly good position. For others it is exceedingly bad. Find out, by actual tests, how well you read, when flat on your back. Then act accordingly.

Do you do much reading when lying down?

How fast can you read in this position? As fast as when you are sitting up? As fast as when standing?

While some of us read pretty well thus, nobody ever reads effectively in the bent-over posture. It cannot be defended. Yet many business men fall into it.

There are other less frequently used bad postures. Slumping in one's chair, especially sidewise slumping, almost inevitably causes circulation difficulties and muscle tensions which lead to eye strain and headaches.

2. Your position relative to the printed page may be wrong in any of three ways:

a. Your eyes may be too close to the type, or

b. Too far from it, or

c. The page may be tilted so that parts of it lie much farther from your eyes than other parts, hence you have to shift your eye adjustment from word to word, thus causing needless strain.

Usually you tend to hold your reading matter at nearly the correct distance. But some people fall into a habit of muscle adjustment which is not in complete harmony with the needs of their eyes. This is particularly true of persons suffering from very slight eye troubles. And unfortunately it is the very slight imperfection of eyesight, particularly in astigmatism, that upsets the reader most violently. Frightful headaches and even melancholias and indigestion are caused by trifling astigmatism that can scarcely be corrected with glasses.

Now I cannot advise you as to your particular eye habits. Leave that to your oculist. And do not go ahead with these exercises unless you are reasonably sure of your eyes.

As for the faulty position of a tilted page, it is most likely to develop when you read very large-paged or very heavy books. The dictionary, encyclopædias, atlas volumes, and many other references books have excessively large pages or else are very heavy. They cause most trouble of this sort.

Be sure to avoid holding them as you hold small books. A tilted rest is best; and best of all is a reading stand or pulpit with a tilted top. As a rule we do not read such works long enough to cause much trouble. But some people do, and must have a care.

Fig. 3.—Bad position as to source of light. Here is positively the worst of all positions with respect to the light. Notice that the young man directly faces a strong light which causes him to squint. Notice also that the page he is reading is wholly in shadow, while the back of the book gets all the light. His eyes adjust so as to read in a very bright light, but what he reads is in the dark. Most of us have been trained to avoid this dangerous habit. But not all of us avoid it as rigorously as we should.

3. Your bodily position relative to the light presents two aspects: (*a*) the way the light strikes the type, and (*b*) the way the light strikes your eyes.

a. There are three wrong ways of illumining the type:

(1) With too intense a light.

(2) With too faint a light.

(3) With very uneven light, so that parts of the page are bright and parts dark.

Fig. 4.—Bad position as to source of light. While we usually avoid facing a bright light while we read, we are not so careful in shunning this almost equally harmful position, in which a bright light strikes one eye, while the other eye is in shadow. As you here see the young man, the page he is reading is moderately well illuminated with a bright but slanting light. His eye that is nearer the light source is directly illuminated, hence the pupil contracts by way of adjusting to vision in bright light. But his other eye is wholly shaded, hence its pupil expands for reading in weak illumination. The page he reads is neither very bright nor very dark. So neither eye is correctly adjusted to it. Eye strain, headaches, and poor comprehension will almost certainly result, if he reads much in this position.

In days of old, before cheap electricity, the tendency was to read in too faint lights. Today the trend is opposite;

most of us who work in large city offices are in constant danger of overbright lights. Recent studies reveal that ordinary work and reading can be done as efficiently in

FIG. 5.—Correct reading position. Here the young man's back is straight, his head slightly inclined but not drooping, and the book page at his own best distance. The light is coming from behind and somewhat above his shoulder, so that it falls on the page evenly. Both of his eyes are in the same degree of shadow. Some people would hold the book a little higher, others would hold it closer, still others further away. But all should hold it in this same *general relation* to light and eyes.

lights much fainter than those generally used in offices and factories. The bright lights have a psychological value, however, in that they seem to stimulate many workers. It is no figure of speech to say that the "Bright

Lights" are jazzy.   Men do speed up when under **bright** lights and slow down under dim ones.

Probably you have no need of being sped up, however. So spare your eyes.   Find out by tests at which degree of

FIG. 6.—Wrong angle between page and eye.   In this reading position, the top line on the page is about twice as far from the eyes as is the bottom line; and every line between top and bottom is at a different distance from the eyes. Hence the eye has to readjust in order to read each line.   This is hard, too hard indeed.   Perhaps you can read fairly well thus.   But why throw a needless load on your eyes?   Think of your eyes as a priceless machine which must be utilized to the utmost.

brightness you read easily.   And then make a practice of shunning brighter lights.

Experiment on yourself.   Try sitting at various distances from a light of known intensity.   Also try reading with bulbs of various wattage at a given distance. When I tried this on myself some years ago, I was amazed to find how little light I needed, in order to keep up the immense reading I do. Many people exclaim at the darkness of my library, and I have to explain that I am not trying to save forty cents a year on my electric current bills.

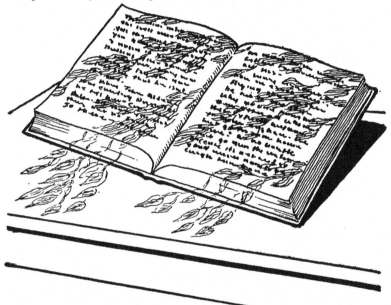

Fig. 7.—Mixed light and shade. This book is on a table under a pergola through whose overhead leaves the sunlight filters down on the reading matter. The contrast between the bright sunlight and the shadow of the leaves is much stronger in reality than in this photograph. You doubtless know from experience how hard it is to read under these conditions.

No two people are alike in this sensitivity. All the more reason for your checking up on yourself with care. Bear in mind that excessive brightness is more likely to prove troublesome than excessive dimness, though at the moment of reading the latter may seem worse.

As for uneven illumination, this can be grave indeed. There are two varieties of it:

(1) Continuously uneven illumination, as when the light falls on the page from far at one side of the reader.

(2) Broken or mottled light, which in turn may be (a) stationary, or (b) moving, with respect to the page.

The first sort is not likely to prove very serious unless at the same time the light happens to strike one eye and not the other. This will be discussed in a moment.

The second sort is always serious, whether light strikes the eyes unequally or not. The stationary mottling of the page caused by a bright light throwing the shadow of a window frame or a lattice or the leaves of a tree on the page so that bright and dark spots or lines alternate across it is most harmful. Why? Because the eye must readjust the pupil several times as it crosses the page; and, as the eye will outrun the pupil in these adjustments, the result is that the retina receives too much and too little light from the spots in quick succession.

One degree worse is the moving figure of light and shadow. You get this whenever you sit under a wind-blown tree in the good old summer time and strive to read with the light that filters through the fluttering leaves. You get it still more obnoxiously whenever you sit on the sunny side of a train and read, holding your book so that the sunlight strikes it, flinging across the page the swiftly moving shadows of telegraph poles and wires, trees, tower houses, and other passing trains.

Though I cannot prove it beyond my own personal experience, I am quite convinced that many business men impair their reading ability for the day by trying to peruse their morning newspapers in this manner. Only a few minutes of such a terrific strain on the eyes is needed to set up tensions and accompanying irritations which will make later reading in the course of the day's work highly uncomfortable. if not slow and inaccurate.

b. There are two importantly wrong ways in which the light may strike the eyes:

    (1) It may shine directly into both eyes from a position back of the page you are reading.

    (2) It may shine into one eye but not into the other, as it comes from a side position.

Of these two, the former is by all odds the more injurious. Why? Because it causes an adjustment of the pupils which is the reverse of correct. Being exposed to direct light, the pupils contract and are then adjusted for seeing objects in bright light. But the page lies in shadow. To read it, the pupils ought to be more or less dilated. Too little light from the type reaches the retina. You might as well be reading in the late dusk. The eyestrain is grave indeed.

The worst of all conceivable relations between body, page, and light would be one in which the illumination shone directly into the eyes and consisted of very bright lights alternating with swiftly moving, irregular shadows such as you might get were you to read a book in an open automobile while driving on a sunny day along a road overhung with shade trees through which the direct sunlight broke.

B. ACTION HABITS

It is hard to generalize about these. The best I can do is to suggest. Some people move rapidly, others slowly, others jerkily. As a result, some do not keep sufficiently still when they read, while others are too still and still others simply fidget.

I once knew a man who read serious matter only when pacing up and down the office, running one hand through his hair while he held the book or paper in a hit-and-miss fashion with the other hand. Naturally he was a slow, as well as an inaccurate, reader.

I also know a woman whose profession requires of her a vast deal of reading. She sits at her desk as motionless as a statue. And then wonders, at the day's end, why she is fairly paralyzed and all pallid around the gills.

Between these extremes you will find your own happy medium of action habits. And that is about all that can be said.

Then too we have the action habits of the eye itself. A man whose business involves a great deal of long-range vision need not marvel at his slow or uncomfortable reading. A civil engineer who spends his day outdoors looking across valleys and up long roads gets his eyes into long-focus habits and also into slow, lateral-motion habits which interfere with the short-focus and fast back-and-forth shift of the eye that reads print.

At the other extreme we find the chronic reader of trash, the person who, usually in childhood, has formed the habit of wading through the funny columns of newspapers and endless cheap fiction. So far, so good. But when such a trash reader grows up and gets into serious business, he finds himself handicapped in reading serious material which must not be so lightly skimmed.

I know a clever man of this type. He is the envy of his friends because of the immense amount of reading he does. He has a large library and regularly sails through all kinds of books, about which he will talk with you glibly. But, alas and alack! whenever I talk with him about some book we have both read, I find that his notions about it are so hazy that he might better never have dipped into its pages. For ignorance is safer than misinformation. When you know nothing, you are at least free to use your own wits in forming some idea; but when you know with profound certainty something that isn't so, you are chained to an error.

This man has the unbreakable habit of moving his eyes faster than he can move his mind. He has a pretty good mind, on the whole, but his eyes are marvelous. He is a very bad reader—one of the worst varieties—simply because he has never been able to drive eyes and brain at the same speed, relative to some given subject matter. He is not even a reliable skimmer, though he thinks himself a marvel. For a good skimmer's mind outruns his eye, as a rule, and grasps large implications of things read, even when the details of the latter have not been taken in through the eye.

Eye skimming is one thing. Content skimming is another. If you wish merely to know what a book or article is about, eye skimming is useful. If you wish to know what the words say, you must skim content.

Is it clear that habits of body and eye can make you a poor reader? And that such a habit that suits one kind of reading may unfit you for other kinds?

Strictly speaking, nobody is a good universal reader. We all specialize more or less as we read more and more of certain sorts of material. One man becomes an adept at reading statistics—which most of us cannot take in fast because we have not drilled ourselves so to do. Another man absorbs the clumsy, bad writing of lawyers and legal documents but is quite unable to attain speed and precision in reading popular scientific articles.

We all know why this is so. The lawyer is familiar with the ideas and terms and manners of the law but not with those of physics and chemistry. The statistician knows his mathematics. Our habits of work form the foundation of our reading habits. And this reveals itself in the make-up of our working vocabulary and in our grasp of technical styles.

Thus we come to the most important of all habits, namely words.

Words are habits.

I do not mean, of course, the printed mark, "Cat." I mean this mark *as a bearer of meanings*. So long as it carries no meaning it is not a word. It becomes a word, as soon as your mind acquires the habit of letting it stand for a small feline that purrs, laps milk, scratches when annoyed, and meows when the spirit moves. The ink on the page simply touches off this habit of meaning in you.

A German forms the habit of being touched off thus when he sees the mark, "Katze." A Frenchman when he sees "Chat."

Any old mark will do. It all depends on what habit you form toward it. We might all agree to substitute for the mark, "Cat," a new mark, "Ubdub." And in the course of time, as fast as we formed a new habit of mental response toward "Ubdub," it would be a genuine word.

Our scientists are doing this all the time. They are finding new substances and processes in physics and chemistry and medicine and bacteriology for which no word has ever existed in any language. They know they will have to form a habit of dealing with these new things, so they must form a habit of referring to them by means of conventional marks, signs, and sounds. To you, who never deal with the things, this often sounds foolish and affected. But it is not.

Physicans today deal with "Klieg eyes," which did not exist until the motion pictures were commercialized some ten or fifteen years ago. They talk about "auriculoventricular extrasystole" simply because somebody happened to discover this particular kind of premature contraction of the heart. Chemists create "dimethylaminobenzaldehyde" in the form of colorless crystalline plates: and then they have to create the word to describe and mean the stuff. Business men are doing the same thing all the time, but they do not sense it so keenly because they usually combine old words into new combinations and give them novel connotations. We talk about "mergers," "the monthly index," "cash registers," "Automats," "a soft market," and a million other things utterly meaningless to people outside of American business.

And when you listen to a radio expert, to an aviator, to an automobile specialist!

Don't they speak a language foreign to you? Yes, of course! Is it English? Only in a peculiar sense. It is the language of men whose habits are built around certain kinds of things and kinds of work. They build this language out of old word-marks used by English-speaking people, while others build theirs out of old word marks used by Germans, French, or Japanese. When an aviator talks about "dollies," he doesn't mean what your little girl does when she uses the same mark. Aviator and girl speak two languages, in reality.

Now, what has all this to do with aiding you to read better?

Simply this. *Fast and Sure Reading is Simply the Act of Grasping the Intended Meanings of Marks on the Printed Page in a Fast and Sure Manner. To Grasp the Meanings, You Must First Have Developed the Habit of Linking Them with the Printed Marks: and to Do This, You Must Know All the Important Meanings Which a Given Mark Can Carry in Different Contexts.*

Most marks carry many meanings. This is the aim of language, to simplify communication by letting one thing stand for many things. When you learn, you usually learn only one or two of its commonest meanings. As you widen your range of experience and reading, you add new meanings.

Which meanings do you select, as you read? Suppose you have learned the common meaning of the little mark, "of." This indicates possession. Thus: "The house *of* my friend, Jones." Later you learn that the same mark also means, in other contexts, the constitution or quality of the prepositional antecedent. Thus: "Jones built his house *of* stone." Still later you find that the mark sometimes indicates origin. Thus: "A woman *of* Paris."

Is it not clear that the only way you can tell which meaning must be selected is first to catch the drift of the whole passage? Or, if this cannot be done, to proceed by eliminating the least likely meanings, one by one, until you hit upon the correct interpretation?

In a sense, then, all reading is a guessing game. If you guess the general subject matter and the drift of the writer's remarks, you readily fit the right meanings to the right marks on the page. And if you cannot guess it, then you are lost.

If you are not versed in industrial chemistry, for example, what can you do with a passage like this?

Eucasin, manufactured by passing ammonia gas over casein, is marketed in technical grades.
Ethylene glycol derives from heating ethylene chloride with sodium formate in methyl alcohol solution.

Or, if you are not a student of aviation, how about this?

This biplane has a strutless design. Its center of gravity is such that high variability in pay load necessitates very slight readjustments in manœuvring. The stabilizer is adjustable from the rear cockpit. All exposed lugs lie in a plane parallel to the slip-stream. No gap occurs where the ailerons join the wings, as there is a dural fairing on the wing and a dural strip rolled over the back of the aileron.

Technical? Of course! But let me emphazise one thing right away. *Nearly All of the Serious Reading Which the Modern Business Man and Manufacturer Must Cover Is Shot Through with Technical Facts. These Facts Are Expressed through Words and Symbols in Their Own Special Way.*

Hence, to Read Them Well, You Must:

1. *Know the Facts.*
2. *Know Their Symbols.*

One reason you may have trouble with your reading is that you never learned the facts in school; another reason is that, after you learned the facts in your business or profession, you did not master their symbols.

You may have a magnificient grasp of the facts alone and still read about them with difficulty. If so, you must start at once building up a habit of word use and word recognition.

The Better Your Vocabulary, the Better You Will Read.

But a Good Vocabulary Does Not Consist Merely of a Set of Words. It Includes Also the Many Various Shades of Meanings These Words Carry in Special Contexts.

Many readers fool themselves about their vocabulary. They think they know, let us say, 40,000 words. But in reality they only know about one-fifth of each of these words; that is, they know some one meaning of each.

A Big Vocabulary Is Not Nearly So Useful as a Moderate One Thoroughly Understood.

It is Much More Useful to Know All the Important Meanings of 15,000 Words than to Know Only One Meaning of Each of 50,000 Words.

Mastery of a Little is Better Than Shallow Knowledge of Much.

One of the commonest causes of poor reading among adults is the habit of reading easy matter. This habit is founded in our schools, which teach us reading by putting into our hands the best writings of the world's greatest masters of literary expression. The vast bulk of serious reading material used in the everyday business of most men and women is produced by writers of average ability or less. Naturally, their books and articles are much harder to read than the masterpieces of Dickens, Thackeray, and Kipling. And this, too, quite apart from the fact that the subject matter of practical reading is always more complex than the subject matter of pleasant fiction.

Our schools still further habituate us to easy reading by teaching us all the other subjects, such as geography, arithmetic, history, civics, etc., through textbooks prepared with the greatest of skill. The clarity and simplicity of the American textbooks is on the whole extraordinary. They are deliberately planned so as to offer the least possible resistance to the teacher in teaching and to the student in learning. Now this is all well and good. Young people ought to learn everything as easily as possible. But if they receive no other drill in reading than such as is offered in literary masterpieces and model textbooks, you may be sure that they will go out into the world quite unprepared to read an engineer's report on some business project or a trade digest of market conditions in iron and steel.

The plain truth is that our grammar-school and high-school graduates must learn to read all over again as soon as they attain responsible positions in the world. So, too, must those of our college graduates whose training has been preëminently cultural.

We come now to two very bad habits which are sometimes related but usually occur in different people separately.

Word Reading

1. Word reading is the habit of looking at each individual word and dwelling too intently upon its own separate meaning. This is likely to result from one of two tendencies: either some childhood difficulty at the time when one learned to read or else, in adult years, to the habit of reading very technical, hard work calling for the closest concentration. The childhood difficulty is hard to over-

come, just as is any other defect of early education or early nature. It can be conquered with effort, though, unless it is caused by some eye defect or poor intelligence.

As nobody who studies this book will suffer from poor intelligence, I shall consider as the one possibility slow eye perception. You can easily test yourself for this.

A normal adult eye takes in four or five ordinary words at a glance. The finest eye in the world cannot take in more than seven. And the worst eye takes in only one, as did a student who once came under my observation. I am speaking, of course, about continued reading. Not about a single act. In some of the tests which follow, you may take in at a glance seven or eight words. But you will be utterly unable to maintain any such rate in actual reading.

If you take in two or three words at once, as you read, you are surely a word reader and will have to do something drastic to improve yourself, if this is at all possible.

First of all, have your eyes examined by an oculist. They may not be receiving a clear image of more than two words at once.

After this possibility has been eliminated, there remains the other one: perhaps you simply have formed a bad habit of looking at words instead of at longer phrases. To test yourself in this respect, work on the exercises which follow. And be very careful about timing yourself well.

Revery Reading

2. Revery reading appears, to an external spectator, to be the same as word reading. But it is not. Here, the central nervous system responds too lustily to the perceived word. The revery reader slows down badly as a result of being too intensely stimulated by words. Images, memories, and emotions flash up superabundantly with

each fresh word or phrase. And his attention shifts from the printed page to these inner responses of the spirit. Hence, he loses the drift and the larger meaning of the text. His mind leaves it, flies all over the universe, and then returns to pick up the lost thread.

To day dream over a page is common in childhood and youth, when all reading is still a delightful novelty. It is very rare among business and professional men. Day dreamers usually fail to rise in the ranks of modern corporations; so we shall here be spared the worry of reëducating them. But there is a minor variety of them that must be mentioned because it occurs among professional workers now and then. It is the scientifically minded person whose interests in the subject being read are both intensive and extensive. He is the genuine student. He slows down simply because he thinks of so much that is relevant to the subject. His mind does not wander as the day dreamer's. Rather does it plunge deeply into things. Instead of advancing, it dives.

Now, this is a fault only in so far as it becomes a fixed habit which prevents the student from rapid reading of material that does not require intensive study. I find some engineers laboring under this handicap, and also some lawyers. Their professional reading habits are all right, but their non-professional reading goes on sluggishly. They do not know how to relax with their eyes and minds. But, luckily, they can learn this. The exercises later given for skimming will start them right.

3. MOMENTARY CONDITIONS OF READING

A. YOUR SURROUNDINGS

Noise.

Unless you are too old, train yourself to read in noisy surroundings. But whenever possible, read where it is quiet. The ability to shut out disturbing stimuli is priceless, but this is no reason why you should always try to exercise it by retiring to a boiler factory for your day's reading. Altogether too many children are coddled by parents and teachers, who place the little darlings in the quiet for their serious studies. I often think the old-style Chinese school is better than ours in this respect. For there, you know, all the pupils learn their lessons by shouting out loud in class.

Air.

Be sure that you do no serious reading in an overheated room. A headache may result; and, if not that, then poor comprehension of the subject matter.

Chill air and draughts may disturb your reading. But they are less likely to do this than heat.

Time of Day.

At which time of day do you read best?

Check up on yourself carefully. Perhaps you know. But it is more than likely that you don't. Few of us ever study ourselves thus.

I happen to be one of those unfortunates who can do no heavy reading after dinner. And I prefer to omit all early morning reading for the sake of other tasks requiring my best efforts. Hence, more or less of necessity, I am strictly a mid-day and early afternoon reader.

Were I to try forcing myself to read important technical or scientific books at night, I should fall asleep over them or else make such sluggish progress that the time would be unprofitably spent.

Possibly you are the reverse, as many people are. To study difficult material before eleven o'clock (in the morning) is impossible for them; and so, too, is all other hard reading.

Whatever your natural and best distribution of reading time happens to be, make the most of it. Avoid trying to alter it, for it is certainly the result of hundreds of old, deeply rooted habits. (This, of course, would not apply to children. I am speaking solely to adults.)

Illumination.

Be sure to have correct illumination when you read.

Eye strain may be caused either by too bright light or too weak light. It may also result from a bad reading position with reference to the source of light.

When you read under an excessively bright light, the pupils of your eyes contract and so do the muscles of the eyelids and the face. These muscle tensions eventually become painful and may cause severe headaches.

If you read in too faint light, another set of annoying muscle tensions develops.

Should you assume a bad reading position relative to the light, one of the commonest ill effects is a different adjustment of each eye to the printed page. For example, your left eye may adjust so as to shut out light while your right eye adjusts so as to take in more. This unbalance can cause extreme discomfort and fatigue.

Fortunately, it is easy to have correct illumination these days. Other things beside the amount of illumination must be considered, however, for easy and comfortable vision. Wrong colors, reflecting surfaces at bad angles, too-bright ceilings, shadows, the wrong kind of work to be done in a given light may all be factors in causing eye strain. Uncovered lights may easily be another source of eye discomfort, although these are not now prevailingly used, particularly in modern offices.

Probably the best form of indirect lighting is a fixture so constructed that the opaque undersurface is indirectly illuminated with a not too-high candle power lamp. More fixtures with low candle power are better for easy vision than one or two with high. The source of light should be so placed that the direct rays do not enter the eye. Otherwise these rays are brighter than the object viewed, causing eyestrain.

Reading Matter.

Paper and Type.—Here are the characteristics of paper and type which make for easy reading:[1]

1. **Size of the Book.**—Smaller books which can be easily held in one hand are preferred. Larger books must usually rest on a support, with the result that the letters are often exposed at an angle, thus greatly lessening their legibility.
2. **Texture of the Paper.**—The paper should be of such a quality that the printing on one side will not show through on the other. Furthermore, the printing on one side of the page must be so done that the evenness of the surface of the other side of the page is not affected.
3. **Color of the Paper.**—The paper should be pure white, inasmuch as the legibility depends in part on the contrast between the black of the printed letters and the white of their background. Furthermore, the surface of the paper should have no gloss, since a glossy surface is especially trying to the eyes.[2]

[1] From the Eighteenth Yearbook, National Society for the Study of Education, Part II, 1919. Fourth Report of the Committee on Economy of Time in Education, 1919. Public School Publishing Company. Bloomington, Illinois. "Suggestions Relating to the Hygiene of Reading."

[2] This statement is correct so far as the standard commercial papers are concerned. But it has been established that there are two types of paper and type combination which afford a much greater contrast than black and white. The best contrast of all is white ink on black paper. This causes the least eye strain because the mass of the page constituting the background of type reflects the least amount of light. Unfortunately, there does not seem to be any way of manufacturing dead black paper cheaply enough to justify such a radical departure from trade practices. The next best combination is dead black type on lemon yellow paper. The amount of light reflected under ordinary conditions of illumination is much greater from lemon yellow than from white. There seems to be no reason why publishers should not put out books on paper of this tint.

4. Color of Type.—The printed letters should have sharp, clear cut outlines and should be deep black.

5. Color of Pictures.—The use of highly colored pictures and drawings is questioned by some investigators. Experiments indicate that peripheral color stimuli may affect the accuracy of fixation and interfere with the accuracy of the reading movements.

6. Length of Lines.—Investigators generally favor the shorter rather than the longer lines. There is a preference for lines between 60 and 80 millimeters in length, with 90 millimeters as a maximum. Experiments show that lines the length of those in the columns of a newspaper can be read more rapidly per unit than lines of greater length.

7. Uniformity in Length of Line.—Huey and Dearborn agree that the lines of a given selection should be uniform in length, because a reader drops quickly into a habit of making a constant number of movements and pauses per line . . .

8. Distance between Lines.—A minimal leading of 2.5 millimeters between lines should probably be required. Increasing the leading does not seem to help. If the letters are undersize, the extra space should be used in increasing the size of the letters . . .

9. Size of Type.—Investigators are generally agreed that eleven point type, about 1.5 millimeters in height for the short letters (m, n, o,) should be made a minimum. Material printed in this size of type is read faster and individual words recognized more quickly than when the type is smaller . . .

10. Thickness of the Vertical Stroke.—The letters should stand out clearly and distinctly. The thickness of the vertical stroke should not be less than 0.25 millimeters, and 0.3 millimeters is preferred by some . . .

11. Space between Vertical Strokes.—The vertical strokes within a letter should be from 0.3 to 0.5 millimeters apart; the vertical strokes of adjacent letters should be from 0.5 to 0.75 millimeters apart.

12. Space between Letters.—Huey states that a minimum of six or seven letters per running centimeter is a convenient approximate guage.

13. Space between Words.—A distance of 2.0 millimeters between words has been generally accepted.

These characteristics best suit school children.   But few adults will fail to find them right.   Donald G. Paterson and Miles A. Tinker have recently tested several hundred college students and find that they read fastest and most accurately when the type size is ten-point and the line length is 80 millimeters. This, you will observe, is almost the same as with young children.[1]

Well-trained men and women, are not easily disturbed by colored pictures, though some are. They can also read, without effort, lines considerably longer than 90 millimeters after a little training. And type smaller than ten-point serves quite as well; but it must not run below eight-point in any case, if maximum ease of reading is sought.

You must keep in mind that economic factors interfere more or less with these ideal rules. To print, for instance, an unabridged dictionary or an encyclopaedia in eleven-point leaded lines of not more than 90 millimeters in length would so increase the size of such works that few people could afford to buy them. And the necessity of making them extremely readable is not great, inasmuch as we seldom read continuously in them for longer than ten or fifteen minutes.

Type like this is too black and thick to be easily read. There is not enough contrast between the letter and its background.

The Major sate down at his accustomed table then, and while the waiters went to bring him his hot toast and his newspaper, he surveyed his letters through his gold double eye-glass. He carried it so gayly, you would hardly have known it was spectacles in disguise, and examined one pretty note after another, and laid them by in order. There were large solemn dinner cards, suggestive of three courses and heavy conversation; there were neat little confidential notes, conveying female entreaties; there was a note on thick official paper from the Marquis of Steyne, telling him to come to Richmond to a little party at the Star and Garter, and speak French, which language the major possessed very perfectly; and another from the Bishop of Ealing and Mrs. Trail, requesting the honor

[1] See, *Journal of Applied Phychology,* Vol. 12, Nos. 4 and 5.

Type like this is too thin and faint to be easily read. In fast action, the eye fails to catch some of the thinner lines and misconstrues the letters.

The major sate down at his accustomed table then, and while the waiters went to bring him his hot toast and his newspaper, he surveyed his letters through his gold double eye-glass. He carried it so gayly, you would hardly have known it was spectacles in disguise, and examined one pretty note after another, and laid them by in order. There were large solemn dinner cards, suggestive of three courses and heavy conversation; there were neat little confidential notes, conveying female entreaties; there was a note on

Type like this is too small to read fast. Avoid it whenever you can.

The major sate down at his accustomed table then, and while the waiters went to bring him his hot toast and his newpaper, he surveyed his letters through his gold double eye-glass. He carried it so gayly you would hardly have known it was spectacles in disguise, and examined one pretty note after another, and laid them by in order. There were large solemn dinner cards, suggestive of three courses and heavy conversation; there were neat little confidential notes, conveying female entreaties, there was a note on thick

Length of Line.

Lines like these are too short to make easy reading. The eye must jump back and forth too fast. Furthermore, too many words have to be broken at the end of the line and hyphenated. And a hyphenated word is considerably harder to read than an unbroken one.

Some people are constitutionally poor readers simply because they are poor visualizers. If you happen to be of this sort, we might as well admit at once that we shall not be able to improve your reading nearly so much as that of most other people. But we can still do something for you. A good vis-

Lines as long as these are hard to follow. The eye loses contact and has to go back and catch it. It is also hard to find where the next line begins. Avoid books and magazines using this unsound typography.

Some people are constitutionally poor readers simply because they are poor visualizers. If you happen to be of this sort, we might as well admit at once that we shall not be able to improve your reading nearly so much as that of most other people. But we can still do something for you. A good visualizer is a person who "sees things in his mind's eye"—that is to say, he forms vivid and distinct images of things which he has seen long after he has been looking at them. An unusually good visualizer will be able to do what a friend of mine does, to the great astonishment of the onlookers. He can tell you the exact position on the page and the approximate position in the book of given sentences which he has read several years back. To be an excellent reader, you need not be endowed with such extraordinary eye imagery. But you must be able to gather the meaning from a printed page without

Lines about as long as those used in this book are the easiest to read, and the type is of the most readable size.

The Best Length of Sentence.

For most people the maximum length of thoroughly easy, natural reading is around 16 words, provided that these fall into subordinate units of 4, 5, or 6 words each which can be taken in as units.

No ordinary person attends naturally and easily to more than five or six words at a single moment.

Here are samples of overlong phrases:

The street, which has been in dire need of repaving ever since the Hylan administration went out, will be badly and expensively repaired this year.

The enterprising publishers of the long, elaborate and highly technical industrial engineering history textbook have announced its forthcoming publication.

Sentences like the following are hard to read chiefly because they are too long. Avoid writers who inflict them on you. And give orders to your office staff to keep their sentences down *under* 16 *words*. If many of the words are unusual or very long, keep the sentences still shorter; down to 10 words, if possible.

1. Considering the technical difficulties of making reliable daily analyses of our product at the ovens, the directors have found it advisable to formulate a trade policy which permits our customers, whenever a shipment of our products turns out to run below specifications, to place a substitute order on a rush-delivery basis without extra charge, we assuming the ordinary liabilities and risks in the entire transaction.

2. Following a conference with the director of personnel, who makes other additional suggestions, it seems advisable, in the light of difficulties that have come up within the Credit Department, to move the head of the Credit Files to another department, and to promote his assistant to the head of that department, a change which will be advantageous both to the bank and to its patrons.

3. The witnesses summoned in the case of *Ransom* v. *Phyles* are not available at the present time, one having gone to California and the other being temporarily incapacitated due to injury during the last week, which makes it necessary to postpone the taking of both depositions until a later date.

4. One of the largest deals this season in the easterly Yorkville section, which has been the scene of exceptional activity by operators and builders since Jan. 1, was closed yesterday with the purchase by Dr. Stuart L. Craig of two choice corner plots, one being the northeast corner of First Avenue and Seventy-second Street and the other the northeast corner of York Avenue and Seventy-ninth Street.

Among long sentences, the least difficult are those which consist of nothing more than a series of short sentences connected by "and" and "but."

Here is a sample:

Trading in crude rubber futures on the Rubber Exchange was dull and the price movement was narrow yesterday, although it opened fairly steady, but the market dipped a little and then closed barely steady with prices in seven deliveries unchanged to 20 points down.

The Value of the Stereotyped Phrase.

Words in familiar groups are easier to attend to than those in unfamiliar groups.

If mere ease of perception is the chief aim of writing, the simple and conventionalized phrasing is best.

In much news writing, this is the case. Unusually "fine writing" is out of place here because the reader merely wants the plain facts as fast and as clearly as possible.

RULE: *In Reporting Aim to Use the Simplest Habitual Phrases. Avoid the Badly Built Habitual Varieties.*

The Usefulness of Short Words.

Short words have this advantage over long. They pack more meaning into a single moment of attention. Hence the reader covers more ground per unit of time.

As meanings they are more *intense* than long words.

Contrast these:

I had a good time at your house last night.	It gave me great pleasure to accept your hospitality yesterday evening.
I don't want to go to the lecture.	The prospect of attending the dissertation is not of an enticing nature.
The beach was crowded.	A motley congregation of hoi polloi was gathered at the surf.

Color of Paper.

While blue is a charming color and may be used for short letters that can be read in a minute or two, it is the worst of all for a book or magazine. It absorbs so much light that the contrast between the black type and the background is feeble. Hence it is easily read only in a very strong light.

Make Your Staff Help You Read!

Do you have to read masses of memoranda and reports submitted by members of your organization? Then advise the writers to adopt the Rules of Easy Reading. This will speed up your own work enormously.

B. MOMENTARY CONDITIONS OF BODY

Muscular Fatigue.

The great majority of people cannot do their best reading directly after strenuous physical exercise. (Note to the busy executive: Never try to read an engineer's report at the nineteenth hole!)

When you feel in great need of exercise, do not do heavy reading. You are in a state of muscular restlessness that will interfere with high concentration.

Hunger.

Never try to read anything important while hungry. You may be the one person in a hundred who can do this efficiently. But the other ninety-nine labor under a vague disturbance which is usually not serious enough to rise into

clear consciousness, but is nevertheless an obstacle to whole-minded attention. Every school teacher is familiar with the child who is either restless or dull or both because he has not eaten any breakfast, or because he came to school in the afternoon without enough lunch. Hunger sets up muscle tensions, first in the stomach, and later in other parts of the body. They almost always interfere with the kinds of tensions which you need which serve to sustain eye attention and mind attention.

C. Momentary Conditions of Mind

The Poor Visualizer.

Some people are constitutionally poor readers simply because they are poor visualizers. If you happen to be of this sort, we might as well admit at once that we shall not be able to improve your reading nearly so much as that of most other people. But we can still do something, for you. A good visualizer is a person who "sees things in his mind's eye"—that is to say, he forms vivid and distinct images of things which he has seen long after he has been looking at them. An unusually good visualizer will be able to do what a friend of mine does, to the great astonishment of the onlookers. He can tell you the exact position on the page and the approximate position in the book of given sentences which he has read several years back.

To be an excellent reader, you need not be endowed with such extraordinary eye imagery. But you must be able to gather the meaning from a printed page without definitely reading every single word on it. The competent reader takes in masses of words and perceives their significance in exactly the same way as you will take in the objects in a room into which you glance. Think of good reading just as you might think of your perceiving such a scene.

Contrast these:

I had a good time at your house last night.	It gave me great pleasure to accept your hospitality yesterday evening.
I don't want to go to the lecture.	The prospect of attending the dissertation is not of an enticing nature.
The beach was crowded.	A motley congregation of hoi polloi was gathered at the surf.

Color of Paper.

While blue is a charming color and may be used for short letters that can be read in a minute or two, it is the worst of all for a book or magazine. It absorbs so much light that the contrast between the black type and the background is feeble. Hence it is easily read only in a very strong light.

Make Your Staff Help You Read!

Do you have to read masses of memoranda and reports submitted by members of your organization? Then advise the writers to adopt the Rules of Easy Reading. This will speed up your own work enormously.

B. Momentary Conditions of Body

Muscular Fatigue.

The great majority of people cannot do their best reading directly after strenuous physical exercise. (Note to the busy executive: Never try to read an engineer's report at the nineteenth hole!)

When you feel in great need of exercise, do not do heavy reading. You are in a state of muscular restlessness that will interfere with high concentration.

Hunger.

Never try to read anything important while hungry. You may be the one person in a hundred who can do this efficiently. But the other ninety-nine labor under a vague disturbance which is usually not serious enough to rise into

Contrast these:

I had a good time at your house last night.	It gave me great pleasure to accept your hospitality yesterday evening.
I don't want to go to the lecture.	The prospect of attending the dissertation is not of an enticing nature.
The beach was crowded.	A motley congregation of hoi polloi was gathered at the surf.

Color of Paper.

While blue is a charming color and may be used for short letters that can be read in a minute or two, it is the worst of all for a book or magazine. It absorbs so much light that the contrast between the black type and the background is feeble. Hence it is easily read only in a very strong light.

Make Your Staff Help You Read!

Do you have to read masses of memoranda and reports submitted by members of your organization? Then advise the writers to adopt the Rules of Easy Reading. This will speed up your own work enormously.

B. MOMENTARY CONDITIONS OF BODY

Muscular Fatigue.

The great majority of people cannot do their best reading directly after strenuous physical exercise. (Note to the busy executive: Never try to read an engineer's report at the nineteenth hole!)

When you feel in great need of exercise, do not do heavy reading. You are in a state of muscular restlessness that will interfere with high concentration.

Hunger.

Never try to read anything important while hungry. You may be the one person in a hundred who can do this efficiently. But the other ninety-nine labor under a vague disturbance which is usually not serious enough to rise into

You step up to a closed door, open it quickly, glance about, and then step out, closing the door. What have you seen in the room? You will be able to enumerate an astonishing amount of its furniture and decorations—probably twenty times as much as you have specifically looked at with concentrated attention. So in the reading of a page—the art consists in taking in the whole situation and imagining accurately what you have not definitely perceived.

This manner of reading must not be confused with skimming, which is a wholly different trick. In skimming, you make no attempt to take in all the details. You aim merely at catching the drift.

The Listening Reader.

There is another type of reader which seems to be very common. He understands words by remembering their sounds. Psychologists believe that he is considerably slower in his reading than the visualizer and much faster than the silent talker.

Many people read in this manner by nature and cannot be trained out of it. Or if they could be trained out of it, we should have to begin with them in their first few years of life. If you happen to be of this type, do not be disappointed if you fail to attain the velocities which some other kinds of readers achieve.

The Silent Talker.

It is something of a misfortune that most of us, as little children, learn to read at about the same time that we learn to talk. Because we are learning these two main language functions during the same primitive years, we tend to link them. Our school teachers encourage this by drilling us in reading aloud. The result is that we become permanently fixed in the habit of "inner speech reading." Reading becomes a variety of talking to our-

selves; and as talking is vastly slower than eye reading,
it retards greatly the reading process.

The commonest outward sign of this variety of reader
is a faint movement of the lips while reading. It is doubtful whether many adults in whom this habit is well formed
can be educated out of it.   On the other hand, considerable
speed and accuracy of reading is possible. Accuracy is
likely to be greater here than speed. That is to say, a
skillful silent talker may never be able to read very much
faster than an average man of his own age and education,
but he stands an excellent chance of retaining the content
of his reading vastly better.

The Talking Reader.

The most unfortunate mortal of all is the talking reader.
He must completely articulate whatever his eye takes in.
No mere vestigial lip movement is enough to fix the
meaning. The operations of his eye and intellect are
slowed down by the far more sluggish throat and tongue
movements. Fortunately, few well-educated adults fall
in this class. Young children and adults of outstandingly
inferior intelligence make up the vast majority of talking
readers. Now and then, however, we do find an exception.
I am certain that his handicap can be at least partly
overcome, though I am far from believing this to be easy
for either this type of reader or for his teacher.

If you have the habit of reading aloud to somebody
or of being read to, give it up at once. This is surely
retarding you in your business reading.

Inevitably you tend to carry over into your office the
throat and mouth habits of oral reading, and thus time
is wasted.

The Eye Reader.

The fastest of all readers is the man who reads wholly or
almost wholly with his eyes and never has to complete

the pronouncing of any words or phrases. Many psychologists insist that he uses his throat and tongue just as the silent reader and the talking reader do. Perhaps he does. But he uses them in a muscular shorthand. Faint and very rapid motor reactions of the larynx are all that he needs. We have excellent proof of this in the fact that many skilled eye readers can read and assimilate material from three to five times as fast as anybody can talk it.

The Distracted Mind.

One of the most useless and annoying of practices is to attempt reading serious material while the mind is fixed on some other object. Millions of hours have been wasted in this futile endeavor. One man in a thousand can turn his undivided attention from one subject to another without effort. But the normal human being cannot shut the door on whatever is strongly interesting him at the moment and plunge into a book dealing with some totally different interest. Serious reading demands a whole mind. Rather than undertake it with half a mind, you might better not read at all. The ancient rule holds true here, "One thing at a time, and do that well."

The busy executive finds this rule one of the hardest to follow. The day's work brings to his desk such a variety of problems and interests!

The Overburdened Memory.

We come now to a wrong reading method which is all too common among men who have to pass on highly technical problems. Lawyers, engineers, production managers, and many others often try to read material dealing with some subject which can be understood properly only when the reader carries clearly in mind a vast mass of facts.

Here we see the need of supporting the memory in order to read with high efficiency. In one sense it is not a prob-

lem of reading. Rather is it a problem of mastering or
having available the background of information which
makes reading profitable. I have seen highly competent
lawyers undertake to read contracts and case records whose
significance went lost because, as they read, they could not
clearly recall various facts and principles which underlay
the subject matter.

The rational procedure here is to look up the necessary
background of information before you read, or else to have
it at your elbow so that you can refer to it, while you read.
Many people never think of this simple trick, because their
reading habits have all been built around easy reading,
for which no such array of supporting facts is needed.

Inaccurate reading is fatal here. Better not read at
all than read without comprehension!

How make such difficult reading as easy as possible?
Organize all that you read in some quickly available
form.

This brings us to the art of keeping notes.

Save the Gist of What You Read!

What I am about to say may not apply to some readers.
But it surely does to nine out of ten.

The time you spend in reading is an investment. You
ought to get good returns on it. But, in order to do so, you
must salt down the essence of books and articles in whatever
form proves most usable.

It is foolish to trust to your memory altogether. Why
overburden that excellent function, when it is much easier to
organize your findings in the form of notes and file records?

Furthermore, *You Strengthen Your Reading Habits as
Soon as You Establish the Deeper Habit of Approaching the
Printed Page with the Determination to Grasp It Well Enough
to Write Down a Brief Report for Filing.*

System in preserving the important contents of what you read cannot fail to make you a better reader, *If You Use What You Thus Save.* It will help little if you merely jot down notes, file them, and then forget them forever.

A notebook is not a miser's sock in which treasure is to be hidden. It is a tool drawer, which ought to be opened daily. So too with filing cabinets and their orderly contents.

Every man chooses his own method of filing material. The method should be determined chiefly by the nature of your subjects and by the kind of use you will make of the notes. An engineer requires a well-analyzed and volum-inous note file. A newspaper man must have one still vaster, but it need not be well analyzed. The manager of a department in a factory may be well served if he has a file with only 30 or 40 topic headings that cover the affairs within his own domain. There is no rule here, you see. You must find what you need.

How use your reading notes?

There are many ways. But let me suggest one that you might not hit upon.

After you have finished, let us say, a magazine article on a given subject, write down your notes. Break these up into whatever topical headings you find useful. Then file them accordingly. As you do so, pull out all the other notes under the same headings and run your eye rapidly through them. *Link Up What You Have Just Read with All That You Have Previously Read on the Same Subject.*

It is almost certain that, as you do this, you will discover new relations, if not new facts. And you will strengthen your grasp on the entire subject.

The more frequently you run through your old notes thus, the surer your mastery of them.

And the better your mastery of them, the easier will be your future reading along these lines. For you will bring

to future pages a better organized mass of information.
You will eventually read faster too.

Office-hour Browsing.

I suspect that many busy executives will laugh at my
next suggestion. I recommend that the executive's office
be turned into a library, that he adopt the ancient and
agreeable habit of browsing, that he dip into magazines,
reports, and books at odd moments whenever two conditions can be fulfilled. First, that he can be undisturbed
even for a few minutes, and second, that he is at the moment
actively interested in learning some particular thing. In
other words, he will read most and read best if his reading
can follow the actual flow of his interests from hour to
hour throughout the day. For most people, this procedure
would prove much more fruitful than the more commonly
adopted one of setting aside certain hours of the day or
evening for serious reading.

Bear in mind that I am speaking only of reading that is
done in connection with the day's work. I am not talking
about the reading of fiction or poetry for the sake of
relaxation. One cause of the unsatisfactory progress which
many executives make in their serious business reading is
their postponing it to the end of the day. They are in the
proper mood for relaxation when they attempt it. Inevitably, they approach it in more or less the same spirit with
which they would approach a popular novel. Is it any
wonder that they find it appallingly dull and heavy going?

Regard your business reading as part of the day's
work. Finish it during working hours. Take it as
seriously as you take the payroll, and, as far as possible,
when you leave the office at the day's end, leave your
business reading there too. I will guarantee that most
of you will increase your volume of reading at least fifty
per cent if you encourage this habit.

Don't let any fake success cult trick you into the pernicious habit of "improving your leisure hours" or "building your fortune" by doing heavy business reading out of office hours.

Interruptions.

Plan your important reading so that you can complete it without being interrupted by telephone calls or personal visits. Few people have a power of concentration sufficient to pick up a broken thread of thought quickly and easily. The more technical and the more novel the reading matter is, the more important continuous and undisturbed perusal. You have no difficulty in maintaining privacy while in conference with an important person. Think of every serious book or article you read as an important person. Usually it has a good deal more to offer you than has the important person.

Fit Your Reading to the Moment.

There is one rule of pleasure reading which can be adapted to business reading. An adult should never read anything in which he is not sufficiently interested to pursue with zest. That is the rule of cultural and pleasure reading. Plainly it cannot be literally carried over into your business office. For you often must read reports that merely irritate you, proposals from salesmen which you know you will turn down before you finish the first hundred words, and such things. But this much is possible.

Read Only What Bears Vitally on Your Most Pressing Tasks from Hour to Hour. Avoid Miscellaneous and Random Reading. Learn to Look Up in Good Books and Magazines and Reference Works New Facts Which May Give You a Broader Basis of Judgment and Action in the Immediate Affairs of Your Office.

What does this really mean? It means that you must relate your reading as intimately as possible to your hourly interests and duties. Then you will read at your best, for your whole "set of mind," as well as your active interest and your desire to know things, will tune in with the words you scan.

Above all, it means that you must avoid reading in fixed daily doses and at fixed daily hours and in fixed books or magazines. This instantly puts books into the class with castor oil and early morning exercises. They taste like medicine, and you come to them with a wry face.

Apply Your Findings to Your Affairs as You Read.

If you will make it a rule to read only what bears on some immediate business interest, you will automatically tend to apply what you read to this interest. And this will prove ideal.

Probably, though, you may have to drill yourself a little in making such applications, especially when reading something that bears only remotely or somewhat indirectly on your practical affairs. Here we can give you no rule of procedure except the very simple one:

As You Read, Stop Every Few Minutes and Ask Yourself the Question: "How Does All This Bear on Me and My Affairs?"

The more systematically you do this, the more easily will you remember what you read, in so far as this is worth while, and dismiss all else as irrelevant.

PART II

HOW TO IMPROVE YOUR WORD HABITS

In a book like this I cannot set exercises suited to the special needs of readers in many fields of industry and trade. I cannot teach the silk salesman the right word habits for things in the silk trade, or the automobile engineer the right word habits for his laboratory reading. The best I can do is to submit sample exercises and ask you to invent your own, drawing on your own specialty for the facts and language symbols.

In the main, I must assume that you have made fair progress with our universal English language. But I must also assume that you have never mastered it. Few are those who have! So I shall first suggest that you test yourself in it. Perhaps you know less here than you think!

Exercise

1. Write down, without consulting the dictionary, all the distinct shades of meaning you can think of for the word "heavy."

2. Now write a sentence or phrase in which "heavy" occurs, each time with a distinct meaning.

3. After you have finished, turn to some dictionary (not a small one!) and see how many meanings you have missed.

4. Finally see in the dictionary how many meanings "heavy" has which are strange to you. Ignore the obsolete meanings of course.

5. Repeat the pattern of this exercise with each of the following words:

heel   out
initiate   of

discharge (the verb)	over
contract (the verb)	wild
mill	will
mince	close
strain (the verb)	seed
straight	rule

NOTE.—If you *know* as many as one-half of the meanings of these words, you have an unusually good grasp of them. If you do not know them well enough to write them down on order but do recognize them when you see them in print, then you have a fair working grasp.

Exercise

In a separate section, beginning on page 64, you will find a list of 1,700 words commonly used. They are not the *most* common 1,700 words; they occur less often.

Work on a few of these words every day for six months. Proceed as follows:

1. Write down the meaning of a word, as you understand it. If you know more than one meaning, write all down.

2. Immediately consult the dictionary, to find out how right you are. *Do Not Wait! The Value of This Verification Depends Largely on Catching Yourself Redhanded in a Mistake.*

3. Mark each word whose meaning you have incorrectly grasped. Come back to it on several following days and write down the right meaning. *This Must Be Done in Order to Break Down Your Old Erroneous Word Habit.*

Exercise

Select from any book or magazine which you regularly read as a part of your business work a list of words having more or less technical meanings. If, for example, you follow Wall Street matters, pick such words as

bucketing	amortization
to cover	rediscount
convertible	junior bonds
refinancing	

Do the same with these, day by day, as with the above described list of 1,700 common words.

To Attain Peak Efficiency in Reading, You Ought to Work through All the Words and Phrases Regularly Employed in Your Own Field. Chemists, Lawyers, Engineers and Physicians Do This as a Part of Their Training. Why Should You Not Be as Thorough in Your Word Habits as They are in Theirs?

Do Not Expect Brilliant Results Here Overnight. But if Your Reading Does Not Improve after Three or Four Months of Word Drill, This Will Almost Certainly Indicate That You Suffer from Other Serious Handicaps.

A WORD LIST TO MASTER

Here follows a list of words taken, with permission, from a famous survey made by Professor E. L. Thorndike, of Teachers' College, Columbia University. For school use he prepared a list of the 10,000 words which appear most often in books and newspapers ordinarily read. I must assume that nearly all adults are familiar with the most common words among these. But probably the less common will offer a little difficulty at least to some who wish to improve their reading habits.

Here are the rarest of the 10,000 words in Thorndike's list. When you have learned all their important meanings you will have the basis of a non-technical working vocabulary. To perfect your business reading, you must next build up your own special vocabulary. As you learn new words here, write them down on the blank pages which follow the printed vocabulary.

Be Sure to Avoid Very Rare Words, Select the Important Terms Only, and Be Sure to Learn All the Important Meanings of Each.

abash
abbot
abject
abridge
absolve
abstinence
abstract
abyss
acceptance
accessory
accommodation
accompaniment
accordance
accost
accumulate
achievement
acid
acquit
acute
adapt
adequate
adhere
adieu
adjacent
adjourn
adjudge
adjust
administer
admonish
adoration
adultery
advancement
advantageous
adverse
adze
affront
afore
afresh
aggravate
aggressive
aghast
agitate
akin
alabaster
alacrity
albeit

alcove
alder
allay
allege
alliance
alligator
allowance
ally
aloes
aloof
alteration
alternate
aluminum
alumni
amain
amateur
ambiguous
ambush
amiss
amity
anarchy
anecdote
anew
animate
animosity
annal
annihilate
antagonist
antic
aperture
apostle
apothecary
appall
apparatus
apparition
appease
appertain
appliance
apprehend
approbation
approximate
arbitrary
arbor
archbishop
archer
archway

arrant
arrogant
arsenal
artisan
ascertain
ascribe
asphalt
aspire
assay
assemblage
assess
assignment
assortment
aster
astray
athwart
atom
atone
attainment
attest
audacious
auger
aught
augment
aurora
austere
authentic
automatic
auxiliary
avalanche
avarice
avenger
axis
aye
azure
babbler
badger
baffle
bail
bale
balk
balmy
ban
bannock
barge
barrette

barrow
barter
baseness
bask
bass
bastard
baste
batiste
battalion
batter
battlement
bauble
bawl
bayonet
beacon
beanstock
bearing (noun)
beck
bedlam
beech
beget
begone
begot
behead
belated
belch
belfry
belie
belle
bemoan
benediction
benefactor
benevolence
benign
benzine
bequeath
beseem
beset
besought
bespeak
bestride
betake
betroth
betwixt
bevel
bewitch

bias	bulwark	chancellor	commodity
bide	bumble	chandelier	commune
bier	bunting	chanticleer	compete
bin	burgess	chaos	compile
binder	burnish	chargeable	complement
bladder	bushing	charger	completion
blanch	butt	chasm	compliance
bland	cackle	chemise	complicate
blaspheme	calomel	cheque	composure
blazon	cambric	chequer	compress
bleak	candid	cheviot	comprise
blemish	candidacy	chide	compulsion
blight	candor	chink	concealment
blithe	canker	chisel	concede
bluster	canon	chivalry	concession
boar	canopy	choleric	concord
bode	canton	chopper	concur
bolster	capacious	chuck	condemnation
bondman	caper	churl	condense
bonus	caprice	cite	condescend
bout	caravan	clamber	conditional
bracket	carbon	clamorous	conduit
brandish	carbuncle	clamp	confessor
brawl	carcass	clan	confide
brawn	carnal	cleaver	confiner
bray	carouse	clemency	confirmation
brazen	carrion	clench	conflagration
breach	carter	clink	confront
breaker	casement	clod	conjugation
brigade	cask	clog	conjunction
brimstone	casque	cloy	conjure
brine	castile	cob	consecration
bristle	castor	cockle	conserve
brittle	caustic	coconut	consistent
broach	cavalier	cocoon	consolation
broider	cavern	coffer	consonant
broil	celluloid	cog	consort
broth	censer	coincidence	conspire
browse	certify	cologne	constable
bruin	chafe	colonel	constraint
buccaneer	challenge	combatant	consul
buck	challis	comer	contemporary
buckle	chamberlain	comet	contention
budge	chambray	commendation	continental
buff	chamois	comment	continuance
bullock	champaign	commodious	continuation

contractor	cue	deride	domain
contrive	cull	descry	don
controversy	curd	desist	dotage
convene	custody	despatch	dote
convict	cycle	destitute	doublet
cope	cymbal	destructive	dower
copperas	damnation	determinate	downy
copse	dangle	devout	dowry
corduroy	dastard	diadem	dram
core	data	diagonal	dreg
corps	daub	dial	dross
corpse	dauntless	dialogue	drought
corruption	dayspring	diameter	dung
corse	daze	dice	dupe
counsellor	dearth	digger	durable
counterfeit	debase	dilapidated	durst
coupling	decimal	dilate	dwindle
cove	declension	diligence	edging
covetous	decorate	dilute	edify
cowl	decoy	diplomat	edition
coy	dedication	discern	efface
cozy	deface	disclaim	effective
craftsman	default	discomfit	eke
crag	defective	discord	elapse
cram	defendant	discount	ell
cramp	defer	discreet	embark
crane	deficiency	disk	embassy
crank	define	dismount	embattled
crate	deform	dispatch	ember
cravat	defraud	dispel	embody
craven	degenerate	displace	emboss
creak	degrade	dissembler	emery
creditor	deity	dissension	eminence
credulous	deliverer	dissipate	emit
creed	dell	dissolution	enact
crevice	delta	dissuade	encamp
crisis	delude	distaff	encompass
crochet	deluge	divers	endue
crock	demeanor	diverse	engender
crucify	demolish	divert	engross
cruise	demon	divination	enhance
cruller	denote	divisor	enjoin
crusade	denounce	divulge	enmity
crystalline	dependant	dodge	ensign
cubit	dependent	dogma	ensnare
cudgel	depute	doleful	entangle

enthrone	fen	frustrate	grinder
enthusiast	fervent	fumble	gripe
entrails	festal	gabble	grit
entrust	feud	gaberdine	grope
envelop	fie	gad	grot
environ	filer	gaiter	grotesque
epic	fillet	galvanize	grovel
epitaph	flange	gamble	gruel
epoch	flank	gambol	guilder
equator	flannel	gape	guile
equipage	flaw	garb	guise
equity	flay	garner	gully
equivalent	flecked	garret	gust
era	fleecy	garrison	hack
eschew	flexible	gaudy	hackney
espouse	flicker	gauge	haddock
espy	flinty	gaunt	hag
essay	floss	gauze	hale
estrange	flounce	gender	halter
ethereal	flounder	gentile	halve
eunuch	floweret	georgette	hanger
evade	flue	gesture	hap
evince	foliage	geyser	harbinger
executor	forbade	girt	hardihood
exempt	forbearance	girth	harmonious.
exert	forcible	glossy	harrow
exhalation	forearm	glutton	harshness
exhort	forecast	gnash	haunch
expand	forerunner	gnat	havoc
expedient	forfeiture	goad	haycock
expend	formation	goblet	hazard
expressive	formidable	gong	haze
extol	fornication	goodman	heather
extremity	forsworn	gourd	hedgehog
exult	fortitude	gradation	hedgerow
fabric	fount	grail	heinous
faction	fowler	granary	hemlock
factor	frailty	grandeur	henceforward
fain	franc	grange	herdsman
falcon	fraught	granulate	hereditary
fallow	fray	graphite	heresy
famish	frenzy	grapple	heritage
farthing	froth	graven	herring
fathom	froward	gravity	hewer
fealty	froze	greenwood	hexagon
felon	frugal	grimace	hickory

hie	impetuous	installment	keel
hillock	impious	insulate	ken
hilt	imply	insure	kilo
hitch	imposition	insurgent	kine
hoar	impotent	integrity	kit
hock	impressive	inter	knead
hod	impute	intercept	knickerbocker
hoist	inanimate	interfere	knoll
homage	incessant	interpose	knuckle
hominy	inclination	intervene	labyrinth
hone	incomparable	intolerable	lading
hoot	incomplete	intricate	ladle
hopper	incubator	intrude	languid
hornet	incurable	intrust	lank
hostage	indent	invader	lapse
hostess	indescribable	invariable	lascivious
hostility	indication	invert	lathe
howbeit	indictment	inveterate	lattice
howsoever	indigo	invigorate	laud
hub	indispensable	invincible	lea
huddle	indolence	invoice	leak
huff	inducement	involuntary	lease
hulk	indulge	iodine	leathern
hull	inestimable	ire	leaven
husbandman	inexhaustible	isinglass	leer
husk	infallible	javelin	legacy
hustle	infamous	jay	legible
hydrometer	infect	jeopardy	legislate
hypocrisy	infest	jerk	lender
hysterical	infidel	jerkin	lens
idolatry	infuse	jig	leper
ignoble	ingenious	jingle	lever
imbibe	inglorious	jockey	levy
immeasurable	ingredient	jocund	lewd
imminent	iniquity	jog	liable
immovable	injunction	jollity	libel
immunity	inlaid	jot	lief
immutable	innovation	jubilant	liege
impair	inoffensive	judicious	linden
impartial	inscribe	jug	lineal
impediment	insertion	jumble	lineament
impel	insight	junction	lint
impend	insinuate	juniper	lisle
impenetrable	insole	junk	loam
imperil	insolence	jurisdiction	loan
imperious	inspect	jut	loathsome

locust	mercerize	munch	obtainable
loft	meridian	mush	occidental
lop	messaline	musk	ode
lore	mete	musket	officious
lotus	metropolis	muskrat	olfactory
lubricant	mettle	muslin	omnipotent
lucid	mica	mustard	onyx
luminous	mien	muster	ooze
lunatic	milch	mutinous	opportune
lute	mince	mutiny	oppressive
luxurious	minion	myriad	optic
macaroon	ministration	myrrh	oral
machinist	minnow	myrtle	orbit
madras	minor	mystic	ordeal
magnanimity	minster	nag	originate
magnet	minstrel	nasal	outcast
maim	miraculous	nationality	outrage
maintenance	mite	nave	oval
malicious	miter	nectar	overbear
mallet	mitigate	negate	overcast
malt	moat	negligence	overlaid
mangle	mocker	negotiate	owlet
manifestation	mold	nestle	packet
manna	molten	nether	pagan
mantel	monotonous	nettle	pageant
manual	monumental	nick	palate
marge	moorland	nipple	palfrey
marker	mop	nomad	pall
marrow	mope	nominate	palpable
marshy	morris	noose	palsy
mart	mortar	notch	pamper
martial	mortify	notorious	panel
massacre	mossy	novice	parable
matin	motley	noxious	paramour
mattock	mottle	nozzle	parchment
maul	moulder	nutmeg	pare
maxim	mouldy	nutting	parley
maximum	mow	oakum	parsley
maze	muck	oblique	particle
meager	muddy	oblivion	partition
mediator	muff	obnoxious	pastoral
meditation	muffin	obscene	patter
medley	muffle	obscurity	patty
meed	mug	obsequious	pawn
menace	mull	observance	pedal
mercenary	mum	obstruction	pedant

peek	pillage	precede	prowess
peerless	pincers	precinct	prowl
pelt	pinion	precipice	publican
pence	pinnace	precise	puddle
pendant	pinnacle	precocious	pug
pendent	piper	predecessor	puller
penetrate	pique	predominant	pulley
penitent	piston	preëminence	pumice
pension	plaid	prejudice	puppet
pent	plaint	prelate	putty
pentagon	plait	premier	quail
penury	pliers	preparatory	quell
peradventure	plod	preposition	quill
percale	plug	prerogative	quince
percolate	plumb	presage	quinine
perdition	plummet	presbyterian	quire
perennial	pluperfect	prescription	quotient
perjure	plush	presidency	radius
pernicious	pod	presumption	raft
perpetuate	poke	pretext	raid
perplexity	pollen	princely	raiment
persecution	pollute	principality	raiser
perseverance	pomegranate	printer	rally
persist	pompous	prior	ramble
personage	ponder	privacy	rampant
perspective	pongee	privy	rampart
persuasion	poplar	proclamation	rape
pert	poplin	prodigal	rapine
pertain	populace	prodigy	rapt
peruse	popularity	proffer	rashness
pervade	porcelain	proficient	ratify
perverse	pore	profile	rational
pest	porridge	profuse	ravage
pestilence	portable	progeny	ravenous
petrify	portal	prologue	ravine
pew	portentous	promenade	ravish
phantom	portiere	promontory	raze
phase	posture	prone	reaper
pheasant	potash	prop	reappear
phoenix	potion	propagate	rebellious
phosphate	potter	propensity	rebound
phosphorus	pouch	prophetic	recede
piazza	pounce	propitious	receiver
picker	prance	prostrate	receptacle
picket	prate	provocation	recessive
pier	precaution	prow	reck

reclaim	retort	salve	sham
recline	retrace	sanction	shamble
recoil	reverberate	sateen	shark
reconciliation	revere	satiate	sharpener
recorder	revert	satyr	shawl
recount	revery	saunter	sheaf
recruit	revile	savor	sheen
rectangular	revolver	scab	sheer
rector	ridden	scabbard	shekel
redeemer	rife	scaffold	shellac
redouble	rift	scaly	sheller
redoubt	rigid	scamper	shelve
redress	rigor	scandal	shew
reef	rind	scoop	shoal
reek	ringer	scope	shod
reflexive	ringlet	scorner	shorn
reformation	rinse	scorpion	shortage
regent	riotous	scrim	shred
regime	risen	scroll	shrivel
reiterate	rivet	scruple	shrug
relapse	rivulet	scullion	shutter
relax	roaster	scum	shuttle
relay	robust	scurry	sickle
reliance	rocker	scythe	sieve
relinquish	rocket	sect	sill
rely	roe	sedate	simmer
repast	role	sediment	simultaneous
repeal	romp	sedition	sinewy
repel	rood	seduce	singe
repentance	rook	seer	sixpence
repine	rosette	seethe	skein
replenish	rosin	seller	skirmish
repress	rout	semblance	skulk
reprobate	royalty	sentinel	slab
repulse	rubbish	separator	slacken
repute	rudder	sepulcher	slam
requite	ruddy	sequel	sleek
resemblance	rue	sequester	sleet
reservation	rumble	seraph	slid
residue	ruminate	serge	slim
respite	rump	sergeant	slime
resplendent	rung	serial	sloth
restitution	russet	server	slug
restorer	saber	settee	slunk
restrict	sachet	sewer	smelt
retinue	salutary	sexton	smitten

smock	steward	surrey	timorous
smother	stifle	sustenance	tincture
sniff	stile	sware	tinder
snip	stirrup	swarthy	tinge
socket	strainer	sweeper	tingle
sodden	straiten	swerve	tinker
solder	strangle	swung	tinsel
solidify	stratagem	sycamore	tint
solvent	stress	sylph	tire
somber	stretcher	sylvan	tit
sonnet	strewn	symmetrical	tithe
sooth	stripling	symphony	tock
sorcerer	strode	symptom	toll
sordid	stronghold	synagogue	toot
sounder	strop	syndicate	topple
species	structure	tabernacle	torpid
specious	strung	tabor	torrid
speck	stubble	taint	trance
specter	stucco	tallow	transact
spick	stud	tanner	transcendent
spicy	sty	tare	transfigure
spike	subvert	taunt	transformer
spilt	successor	tawny	transgress
spiral	succor	teat	transient
spleen	suckle	teem	transit
spoiler	sue	teller	transmission
sportive	sufferance	temperament	travail
spout	suite	tempestuous	treble
sprawl	sully	temporal	tremulous
spreader	sultry	tempter	trend
spree	summary	tenor	trespass
sprig	sumptuous	tension	tribulation
sprightly	sunder	terminal	tribunal
sprite	sundry	terrestrial	trickle
squall	sup	testament	triple
staple	superfluity	tester	trivet
stark	superiority	tether	trivial
stationary	supplant	texture	trodden
stationery	supple	thatch	troth
statute	suppliant	thrall	trowel
stave	supplicate	throb	troy
stealth	supremacy	throttle	truant
stench	surety	thunderbolt	truce
sterile	surfeit	thwart	trudge
sterling	surmise	tilt	trump
stew	surmount	timbrel	trundle

tuft	vane	vintage	whisker
tumbler	vantage	virtual	whit
tumultuous	variable	visage	whiz
turban	variegated	vise	whoop
turbulent	vassal	visitation	whore
turnpike	vat	voile	wick
turret	vaunt	volley	widen
tweed	vehement	volt	wield
twill	veneer	voluptuous	wight
udder	venison	vouch	wile
ulster	venom	vulture	wist
uncouth	vent	waft	woeful
undaunted	venturous	wallet	woodbine
undefiled	verdant	wallow	woof
unerring	verdure	wampum	worsted
unfeigned	vermin	wane	wot
unfurl	vernal	wantonness	wrangle
unscrupulous	vertical	watt	wrathful
untrod	vesper	weal	wrest
upholster	vestal	wean	wringer
upland	vesture	weasel	writhe
usage	via	weaver	wroth
usurp	vial	weld	yew
usury	vicar	welt	yond
utility	victual	wench	yore
uttermost	viewless	wend	zephyr
vacillate	vigilance	whelp	zest
vail	vigorous	whim	zoölogical
valve	villa	whisk	

PART III

HOW TO IMPROVE YOUR EYE GRASP

Warning! Do Not Look at the Following Pages Except under Test Conditions. If You Do Look at Them Accidentally, You Will Have to Ask Somebody to Prepare Another Set of Phrases to Be Used in Testing Your Skill of Perception.

EXERCISES IN HIGH-SPEED READING OF PHRASES

The purpose of these exercises is to show you how many words your eye takes in at a single glance.

The success of the test depends entirely upon your own skill in reducing your look to a single glance. You will get the best results if you will let somebody else operate the cardboard for you.

The method of the test is as follows:

Your assistant is to procure a piece of stiff cardboard about as large as a page of this book. When you are ready for the test, he is to make three or four practice trials on you, using the first exercises. This is merely to enable both of you to become accustomed to the procedure.

The book is to be set up on a desk in some convenient position. Your assistant is to cover the page on which the exercise is printed with the cardboard. You are to look steadily at a point close to the middle of the page thus covered. Your assistant is to ask you when you are ready to look at the printed matter. When you say "Ready," he is to expose the printed matter for the shortest possible period. He ought to be able to slip the cardboard aside and replace it in a fraction of a second.   If he cannot do this, the experiment is a failure.

Perhaps the easiest way for him to make a rapid exposure is to hold the cardboard so that one edge of it barely covers the printed matter.   He will then move the cardboard a very short distance back and forth.

Repeat to your assistant what your eye takes in.   He will then keep any convenient record of your accuracies.

ON THE GREEN BOUGH

WHILE THE SNOW IS FLYING

ON THE ROAD TO WICKHAMSHIRE

ON THE VERGE OF BLOODY REVOLUTION

AS THE GREEK CONFERENCE CLOSED

NEAR THE WINDMILL IN THE COUNTRY

WHOSE TAIL WAS SECURELY AND PAINLESSLY
TIED

SUCH A CURIOUS INTEREST IN CRIMSON TIES

AMONG WHICH THE MUMPS WAS MOST
EMBARRASSING

FINDING THIS INCREASE OF INTEREST TO BE
HIGHLY SIGNIFICANT

AT THE END OF WHICH WAS NARY A RAINBOW

ON THE BACK AND NOSE OF THE SPOTTED CAT

OF WHICH NO MENTION NEED BE MADE AT THIS
TIME

IN SPITE OF THE LACK OF A LARGE MAJORITY VOTE

TO BE HAD FROM WHOSE LONG PAGES MUCH
CONCENTRATED EFFORT

CUSTOMS DECLARATIONS CAUSE UNAVOIDABLE
MISUNDERSTANDINGS AMONG DISTRESSING
CONTROVERSIES ALL OF WHICH LEAD TO
MORE TROUBLE THAN THE COLLECTED
TARIFFS ARE EVER WORTH

REVERSAL OF BIOLOGICAL TYPE IS ASSERTED
TO HAVE OCCURRED DURING SEVERAL GEO-
LOGICAL ERAS, PRODUCING ODD MIXTURES
OF MARSUPIALS WITH OTHER HITHERTO
DISTINCT GENERA

HOW MUCH DO YOU GRASP AND RETAIN?

Could we get you in a laboratory, it would be easy enough to measure your span of comprehension. But as things are, you will find this an exceedingly difficult problem.

So much depends upon your knowledge of the content. And nearly as much depends upon your habits of skimming.

In a test I gave recently, the material used was a clearly written, straightforward, and untechnical description of the developing of a banana plantation. I chose this because the subject was strange to all readers tested.

A seasoned newspaper editor read this at the rate of 7.2 words per second—which is very fast. A young engineer of exceptional thoroughness read it at the rate of only 3.3 words per second. And a cub reporter read it at the rate of 4.7 words per second. The engineer, reading slowly, retained and grasped more facts per hundred words than anybody else. But because he read so little per minute, his total score of facts reported afterward was low. On the other hand, he comprehended the important facts best and paid little heed to petty details. But the cub reporter retained so many of the latter that he missed some of the broader, more significant aspects of banana plantations. The editor's record was intermediate.

Here you see the two extremes of reading—the slow, but thoroughly comprehending, and the fast, well memorized, but poorly organized.

Certainly the business man and the professional man must take the engineer as their model. Better slow and sure, if the price of speed is superficiality.

HOW TO ESTIMATE YOUR GRASP

Here are four samples. Light, average, solid, and heavy. Read each at your ordinary natural rate. Put the book aside and write (or dictate) the facts you have read, stating the most important first. Cast every fact into the form of a declarative sentence. And do not score any one which you cannot so report.

In appraising your reading ability, keep in mind that a ten-year-old boy of average intelligence can recall eight items in an easy newspaper paragraph which he has read only once. This does not mean that he recalls eight complete statements. It means that he recalls eight items in whatever is reported in the news item. One item may be a name, another may be a date, a third may be a remark made by somebody, and so on. His eight items may fail to convey the essential meaning of the paragraph, but as items they are correct.

To measure yourself against him, you ought to count the items in each statement which you remember. For example, if you recall, from one passage, that "President Coolidge returned to the White House yesterday morning," you should score it as three items, namely: (1) President Coolidge, (2) returned to the White House; and (3) yesterday morning.

For convenience, you may reckon such a newspaper paragraph as 75 words long.

Exercise 1[1]

One fine morning in the fall London season, Major Arthur Pendennis came over from his lodgings, according to his custom, to breakfast at a certain club in Pall Mall, of which he was a chief ornament. As he was one of the finest judges of wine in England, and a man of active, dominating, and inquiring spirit, he had been very properly chosen to be a member of the committee of this club and indeed was almost the manager of the institution; and the stewards and waiters bowed before him as reverentially as to a duke or a field-marshal.

---

[1] THACKERAY, WILLIAM MAKEPEACE, "Pendennis," Chap. I.

At a quarter past ten the major invariably made his appearance in the best blacked boots in all London, with a checked morning cravat that never was crumpled until dinner time, a buff waistcoat which bore the crown of his sovereign on the buttons, and linen so spotless that Mr. Brummel himself asked the name of his laundress, and would probably have employed her, had not misfortunes compelled that great man to fly the country. Pendennis' coat, his white gloves, his whiskers, his very cane, were perfect of their kind, as specimens of the costume of a military man *en retraite*. At a distance, or seeing his back merely, you would have taken him to be not more than thirty years old: it was only by a nearer inspection that you saw the factitious nature of his rich brown hair, and that there were a few crows'-feet round about the somewhat faded eyes of his handsome mottled face. His nose was of the Wellington pattern. His hands and wristbands were beautifully long and white. On the latter he wore handsome gold buttons given to him by his Royal Highness the Duke of York, and on the others more than one elegant ring, the chief and largest of them being emblazoned with the famous arms of Pendennis.

He always took possession of the same table in the same corner of the room, from which nobody ever now thought of ousting him. One or two mad wags and wild fellows had in former days, and in freak or bravado, endeavored twice or thrice to deprive him of this place; but there was a quiet dignity in the major's manner as he took his seat at the next table, and surveyed the interlopers, which rendered it impossible for any man to sit and breakfast under his eye; and that table—by the fire and yet near the window—became his own. His letters were laid out there in expectation of his arrival, and many was the young fellow about town who looked with wonder at the number of those notes, and at the seals and franks which they bore. If there was any question about etiquette, society, who was married to whom, of what age such and such a duke was, Pendennis was the man to whom every one appealed. Marchionesses used to drive up to the club, and leave notes for him or fetch him out. He was perfectly affable. The young men liked to walk with him in the Park or down Pall Mall; for he touched his hat to every body, and every other man he met was a lord.

The major sate down at his accustomed table then, and while the waiters went to bring him his hot toast and his newspaper, he surveyed his letters through his gold double eye-glass. He carried it so gayly, you would hardly have known it was spectacles in disguise, and examined one pretty note after another, and laid them by in order. There were large solemn dinner cards, suggestive of three courses and heavy conversation; there were neat little confidential notes, conveying female entreaties; there was a note on thick official paper from the Marquis of Steyne, telling him to come to Richmond to a little party at the Star and Garter, and speak French, which language the major possessed very perfectly; and another from the Bishop of Ealing and Mrs. Trail, requesting the honor of Major Pendennis's company at Ealing House, all of which letters Pendennis read gracefully, and with the more satisfaction, because Glowry, the Scotch surgeon, breakfasting opposite to him, was looking on, and hating him for having so many invitations, which nobody ever sent to Glowry.

These perused, the major took out his pocket-book to see on what days he was disengaged, and which of these many hospitable calls he could afford to accept or decline.

He threw over Cutler, the East India Director, in Baker-street, in order to dine with Lord Steyne and the little French party at the Star and Garter—the bishop he accepted, because, though the dinner was slow he liked to dine with bishops—and so went through his list and disposed of them according to his fancy or interest. Then he took his breakfast and looked over the paper, the gazette, the births and deaths, and the fashionable intelligence, to see that his name was down among the guests at my Lord So-and-So's fete, and in the intervals of these occupations carried on cheerful conversation with his acquaintances about the room.

Among the letters which formed Major Pendennis's budget for that morning there was only one unread, and which lay solitary and apart from all the fashionable London letters, with a country postmark and a homely seal. The superscription was in a pretty, delicate female hand, and though marked "Immediate" by the fair writer, with a strong dash of anxiety under the word, yet the major had, for reasons of his own, neglected up to the present moment his humble rural petitioner, who to be sure could hardly hope to get a hearing among so many grand folks who attended his levee. The fact was, this was a letter from a female relative of Pendennis, and while the grandees of her brother's acquaintance were received and got their interview, and drove off, as it were, the patient country letter remained for a long time waiting for an audience in the ante-chamber under the slop-basin.

At last it came to be this letter's turn, and the major broke a seal with "Fairoaks" engraved upon it, and "Clavering St. Mary's" for a post-mark. It was a double letter, and the major commenced perusing the envelope before he attacked the inner epistle.

"Is it a letter from another *Jook?*" growled Mr. Glowry, inwardly, "Pendennis would not be leaving that to the last, I'm thinking."

"My dear Major Pendennis," the letter ran, "I beg and implore you to come to me *immediately*,"—very likely, thought Pendennis, and Steyne's dinner to-day—"I am in the very greatest grief and perplexity. My dearest boy, who has been hitherto every thing the fondest mother could wish, is grieving me *dreadfully*. He has formed—I can hardly write it—a passion, an infatuation,"—the major grinned—"for an actress who has been performing here. She is at least twelve years older than Arthur—who will not be eighteen till next February—and the wretched boy insists upon marrying her."

"Hay! What's making Pendennis swear now?"—Mr. Glowry asked of himself, for rage and wonder were concentrated in the major's open mouth, as he read this astounding announcement.

"Do, my dear friend," the grief-stricken lady went on, "come to me instantly on the receipt of this; and as Arthur's guardian, entreat, command, the wretched child to give up this most deplorable resolution." And, after more entreaties to the above effect, the writer concluded by signing herself the major's "unhappy affectionate sister, Helen Pendennis."

"Fairoaks, Tuesday"—the major concluded, reading the last words of the letter—"A d—d pretty business at Fairoaks,

Tuesday; now let us see what the boy has to say;" and he took
the other letter, which was written in a great floundering boy's
hand, and sealed with the large signet of the Pendennises, even
larger than the major's own, and with supplementary wax
sputtered all round the seal, in token of the writer's tremulousness
and agitation.

The epistle ran thus—

"Fairoaks,
"Monday, Midnight.

"My Dear Uncle,

"In informing you of my engagement with Miss Costigan, daughter
of J. Chesterfield Costigan Esq., of Costiganstown, but, perhaps, better
known to you under her professional name of Miss Fotheringay, of the
Theaters Royal Drury Lane and Crow-Street, and of the Norwich and
Welsh Circuit, I am aware that I make an announcement which cannot,
according to the present prejudices of society, at least, be welcome to my
family. My dearest mother, on whom, God knows, I would wish to
inflict no needless pain, is deeply moved and grieved, I am sorry to say,
by the intelligence which I have this night conveyed to her. I beseech
you, my dear sir, to come down and reason with her, and console her.
Although obliged by poverty to earn an honorable maintenance by the
exercise of her splendid talents, Miss Costigan's family is as ancient and
noble as our own. When our ancestor, Ralph Pendennis, landed with
Richard II, in Ireland, my Emily's forefathers were kings of that
country. I have the information from Mr. Costigan, who, like yourself, is a country man.

"It is in vain I have attempted to argue with my dear mother, and
prove to her that a young lady of irreproachable character and lineage,
endowed with the most splendid gifts of beauty and genius, who devotes
herself to the exercise of one of the noblest professions, for the sacred
purpose of maintaining her family, is a being whom we should all love
and reverence, rather than avoid; — my poor mother has prejudices
which it is impossible for my logic to overcome, and refuses to welcome
to her arms one who is disposed to be her most affectionate daughter
through life.

"Although Miss Costigan is some years older than myself, that
circumstance does not operate as a barrier to my affection, and I am
sure will not influence its duration. A love like mine, sir, I feel, is con-
tracted once and for ever. As I never had dreamed of love until I saw

her—I feel now that I shall die without ever knowing another passion. It is the fate of my life. It was Miss C.'s own delicacy which suggested that the difference of age, which I never felt, might operate as a bar to our union. But having loved once, I should despise myself, and be unworthy of my name as a gentleman, if I hesitated to abide by my passion: if I did not give all where I felt all, and endow the woman who loves me fondly with my whole heart and my whole fortune.

"I press for a speedy marriage with my Emily—for why, in truth, should it be delayed? A delay implies a doubt, which I cast from me as unworthy. It is impossible that my sentiments can change toward Emily—that at any age she can be anything but the sole object of my love. Why, then, wait? I entreat you, my dear uncle, to come down and reconcile my dear mother to our union, and I address you as a man of the world, *qui mores hominum multorum vidit et urbes,* who will not feel any of the weak scruples and fears which agitate a lady who has scarcely ever left her village.

"Pray come down to us immediately. I am quite confident that— apart from considerations of fortune—you will admire and approve of my Emily.

"Your affectionate Nephew.

"Arthur Pendennis, Jr."

When the major had concluded the perusal of this letter, his countenance assumed an expression of such rage and horror that Glowry the surgeon-official, felt in his pocket for his lancet, which he always carried in his card-case, and thought his respected friend was going into a fit. The intelligence was indeed sufficient to agitate Pendennis. The head of the Pendennises going to marry an actress ten years his senior—a headstrong boy going to plunge into matrimony. "The mother has spoiled the young rascal," groaned the major inwardly, "with her cursed sentimentality and romantic rubbish. My nephew marry a tragedy queen! Gracious mercy, people will laugh at me so that I shall not dare show my head!" And he thought with an inexpressible pang that he must give up Lord Steyne's dinner at Richmond, and most lose his rest and pass the night in an abominable tight mail-coach, instead of taking pleasure, as he had promised himself, in some of the most agreeable and select society in England.

And he must not only give up this but all other engagements for some time to come. Who knows how long the business might detain him. He quitted his breakfast table for the adjoining writing-room, and there ruefully wrote off refusals to the marquis, the earl, the bishop, and all his entertainers; and he ordered his servant to take places in the mail-coach for that evening, of course charging the sum which he disbursed for the seats to the account of the widow and the young scape-grace of whom he was guardian.

Exercise 2[1]

The special training of the public speaker must rest upon the broad foundation of a liberal education. How often the expert engineer, chemist, manufacturer or retailer gives a dry-as-dust speech. He has dug deep into his subject, but has little knowledge of his audience, of human nature. He lacks the warmth, the expansiveness, the intimate and enjoyable contact with men and women, that comes from interest in subjects and ideas comparatively remote from his bread-and-butter occupation. The specialist frequently seems a vacuum when in the company of those not engaged in his kind of study. He has not learned how to be interested in persons and how to interest them. The experienced traveler is usually a good companion. Travel in the world of ideas, in the experiences of men of genius, of humor, of charm and sympathy, of good sense and sober learning, makes one still more adaptable and understanding, more at home, and more welcome in every company. Flexibility and growth are the distinguishing traits of a soundly trained mind.

Human Interest.—Huxley was a great scientist and a fine public speaker. He gave fascinating descriptions and explanations of the doctrine of evolution to enthusiastic audiences of workmen. His printed speeches are widely read today. They have a simplicity, directness and energy that make them models of style. Huxley knew how to tell, how to teach and inspire, because his scientific curiosity touched eagerly everything that is of interest to man. That is what Cicero meant when he said

[1] HOFFMAN, WILLIAM G., "Public Speaking for Business Men," p. 76 ff., McGraw-Hill Book Company, Inc., 1923.

that the orator must be acquainted with all the arts and sciences. Among business men today we have many good speakers, and you will note that almost without exception they have, besides their business, many other resources of stimulating talk.

The Force of Habit.—But whether we intend to be speakers or not, this active, widely ranging attention to the world in which we all live, is necessary for the exercise of our more intelligent thinking. The psychologist tells us that man's mind, like that of the animals, is naturally indolent. Thinking is hard work. The employer corroborates this in his assertion that most employees stop growing after two or three years' familiarity with the job. The mind is simply a collection of habits. Habit is repetition that has become mechanical. One operates a typewriter or a sewing machine automatically. And this is the most economical, efficient way. But this habit-forming tendency invades the upper reaches of thought as well. Teachers fail to grow, says Thorndike, after five or six years of experience. Familiarity makes less and less demand upon our conscious attention, and the grooves of habit are dug deeper and deeper. All of us are in greater or less degree victims of our habits. We need to form the best habit of breaking through the crusts of unintelligent, habitualized thinking. So get interested in something different or get a fresh grip on the old, examine it more consciously. Open the mind, renovate it and don't seal it again. Nothing is final. Keep your senses pleasurably alert and receptive to new impressions, new truth. Life is an adventure, not a story that is told.

Sources of Ideas.—We get our ideas from our environment— our companions, books, neighborhood, and occupation. They make us what we are. They give us our "set" of mind, our attitudes and prejudices. The criminal can with considerable justice blame society for what he is. So can the judge, the lawyer, and everybody else. But we can often modify our environment or leave it for a better one. Education is the greatest force in bringing this about.

What to Read.—Books are wonderful in making a magic and yet a very real environment. Those who speak to us through them are more intimate and have more influence over us than our living companions. "Tell me what you read," observed Goethe, "and I will tell you what you are." Because our experience is so limited and because books interpret the experiences of thousands of years, we naturally learn most from them. Carlyle says, "The true university of these days is a collection of books, and all education is to teach us how to read."

Centuries ago Bacon complained that of the making of books there is no end. Today the condition is immeasurably more appalling and bewildering. Yet we must choose rightly the books needed for our nourishment and learn to use them skilfully.

Do not plod through one book or a collection of books just because they have been highly recommended to you or have deservedly world-wide reputation. Many ambitious readers have suffered mental indigestion and permanent discouragement from books unsuited to their nature or stage of development. The first requirement of profitable reading is interest—as it is of all education. If the words fail to hold your active attention, if they bore you, the book is not for you. Of course you must give a book a reasonable trial. Even if the first chapter is a little painful, the second may strike a spark that may generate a lasting fire of enthusiasm. But in the high schools and colleges many students have acquired an everlasting dislike for the finer types of drama, essay, poetry, and fiction simply because their immature minds were not ready to grapple with the humor, the irony, the philosophy, the reflections of maturity. Years of experience, of disillusion, of suffering and renewed faith are sometimes necessary for the comprehension and realization of the commonplace truths of the copybook. But even trained, educated readers differ widely in tastes and prejudices. To one, Dostoiefsky is a neurotic, a diseased, hopeless subject for the pathologist; to another, a torch of light and warmth. Just as our natures differ, they demand different nourishment, and you yourself must be the one to prescribe. Only sympathetic communion with great minds as revealed in their best books can give you the larger understanding, the perspective, that is a part of culture.

Two Kinds of Books.—Books are readily separated into two classes, those of information and those of inspiration. De Quincey has put this distinction most effectively in a famous passage. He says:

There is the literature of knowledge and there is the literature of power. The function of the first is to teach; the function of the second is to move. The first is a rudder; the second, an oar or a sail. The first speaks to the mere discursive understanding; the second speaks, ultimately it may happen, to the higher understanding or reason, but always through affections of pleasure and sympathy.

What do you learn from "Paradise Lost"? Nothing at all. What do you learn from a cookery-book? Something new—something that you did not know before, in every paragraph. But would you therefore put the wretched cookery-book on a higher level of estimation than the divine poem? What you owe to Milton is not any knowledge, of which a million separate items are still but a million of advancing steps on the same earthly level; what you owe is power, that is, exercise and expansion to your own latent capacity of sympathy with the infinite, where every pulse and each separate influx is a step upwards—a step ascending as upon a Jacob's ladder from earth to mysterious altitudes above the earth. All the steps of knowledge, from first to last, carry you further on the same plane, but could never raise you one foot above your ancient level of earth: whereas the very first step in power is a flight—is an ascending movement into another element where earth is forgotten.

Ruskin may help you to realize this passage a little more fully. In an address to an audience of mechanics and other practical workers (see "Sesame and Lilies") he said:

Books are divisible into two classes,—the books of the hour, and the books of all time.

The good book of the hour, then,—I do not speak of the bad ones—is simply the useful or pleasant talk of some person whom you cannot otherwise converse with, printed for you. Very useful often, telling you what you need to know; very pleasant often, as a sensible friend's present talk would be. These bright accounts of travels; good-humored and witty discussions of questions; lively or pathetic story-telling in the form of a novel; firm fact-telling, by the real agents concerned in the events of passing history;—all these books of the hour, multiplying among us as education becomes more general, are a peculiar possession of the present age. We ought to be entirely thankful for them, and entirely ashamed of ourselves if we make no good use of them. But we make the worst possible use if we allow them to usurp the place of true books; for strictly speaking, they are not books at all, but merely letters or newspapers in good print.

The book of talk is printed. Why? Because its author cannot speak to thousands of people at once; if he could he would—the volume is mere multiplication of his voice . . . But a book is written not *to* multiply the voice merely, not to carry it merely, but to perpetuate it. The author has something to say which he perceives to be true and useful, or helpfully beautiful . . .

Whatever bit of a wise man's work is honestly and benevolently done, that bit is his book, or his piece of art. It is mixed always with evil fragments,—ill done, affected, redundant work. But if you read rightly, you will easily discover the true bits, and those *are* the book.

Now books of this kind have been written in all ages by their greatest men, by great readers, great statesmen, and great thinkers. These are all at your choice; and Life is short. You have heard as much before; yet have you measured and mapped out this short life and its possibilities? Do you know, if you read this, that you cannot read that; that what you lose today you cannot gain tomorrow? Will you go and gossip with your housemaid or your stable-boy when you may talk with queens and kings; or flatter yourselves that it is with any worthy consciousness of your own claims to respect that you jostle with the hungry and common crowd for entree here, and audience there, when all the while this eternal court is open to you, with its society wide as the world, multitudinous as its days—the chosen and the mighty of every place and time?

Get Acquainted.—Read to get acquainted with the world about you. The newspapers and magazines can give you only a superficial view, usually distorted and often incorrect. Read the men and women who are thoughtfully studying and grappling with the profound problems left by the World War. These are perhaps the most critical days in the world's history. Other great wars affected only limited areas. Even the quarter of a century struggle of the French Revolution and the Napoleonic Wars affected only Europe. America, Asia, and Africa looked upon it with the interest of spectators at a play. Today these continents are only a little less profoundly disturbed than Europe. We cannot escape the influence of thought and action thousands of miles away. Isolation for country or for individual is no longer possible. Do not confine yourself to American and English authors.

Reading Lists.—The book review sections of the Sunday *New York Times*, the Saturday *New York Evening Post*, and other well-known newspapers often will give you valuable suggestions for reading. Reading about books is sometimes characterized as a waste of time, but the famous critics and essayists often introduce books to us so attractively that we are tempted to read them. Make reading lists for yourself. Promise to read certain books in the next three months or six months or year. History, science, fiction, philosophy, and poetry mean much to you in a practical way. Napoleon said historians are liars, and Henry Ford characterizes history as "bunk," but if the world had only studied its history as intelligently, as practically, as it studies business, it might have been spared the calamities in which it wallows today. If you wish to see a panorama of the ages, to hear the story of man who slowly evolved from the fish—not another fish story—and now aspires to the stars, read the fascinating narrative of H. G. Wells in "The Outline of History." It will help you to get your bearings in the world. The best of our present-day writers will show you the way to the delightful reading of the masters of the past. You will be struck by the fact that our life has its roots deep down in the generations forgotten as "bunk." Abraham, Confucius, Socrates, Shakespeare, and Lincoln were gentlemen, who would have had no difficulty, as Samuel Crothers has said, in understanding one another.

Biography.—Biography is one of the most practical fields of study for the public speaker. Nothing is of keener interest to audiences than the stories of how great men met the difficulties of living. We are always more interested in people than in things. Biography throws a warmer and more penetrating light upon history. Its gossip makes the past real and near.

Vocational Reading.—The broad-minded man must be sharpened to the point required for scratching a living. Whether he is a teacher, lawyer, doctor, or business man he must be abreast of the theory and practice of his occupation. He must have not only skill in living, but in getting his living. He will have a library of his business, he will be familiar with the trade journals, house organs, and other papers of his craft or profession. This paragraph might be taken for granted were it not for the fact that probably the majority of professional men do little reading about the theory, philosophy, or practice of their vocations after they have graduated from the schools. Their own experience and contact with others in the same work become their only guides. These are most important, to be sure, but they are so close to everyone that it is sometimes hard to see the forest for the trees. At the end of this chapter are short lists of books and magazines which will yield excellent material for talks with friends or to clubs or classes.

How to Read.—This brings us to the question, How to read? Francis Bacon in his essay "Of Studies" says: "Read not to contradict, nor believe, but to weigh and consider." Most readers, if they understand at all, give themselves up completely to the author. One should, of course, give him a sympathetic reading, try to understand his point of view, but not believe him until the thought has been examined in the light of one's own experience. Almost everybody is in awe of print. The use of the word "propaganda" during the War and since has done much to mitigate this tyranny of books and papers. What one reads is not necessarily so.

Challenging "Facts."—This is especially true of chains of reasoning. In such instances the reader owes it to his self-respect to challenge, refute or approve the logic—to be reasonably sure the writer has established his case. Even facts, for which we have to depend upon observers and students from all over the world, can be reported to prove contradictory ideas. "Figures don't lie, but liars can figure." Many "facts" are not facts at all. Many arguments, many speeches, are based upon such facts—upon unsound premises, upon things taken for granted that need close examination. The reader or listener is seldom attentive enough to introductory paragraphs or remarks. If these are accepted without thought, the whole of a false plea or doctrine or argument will often be accepted. G. K. Chesterton in his lecture, "The Ignorance of the Educated," quotes Artemus Ward, who said, "The trouble with people is they know too many things that ain't so." We talk of "half-baked ideas." They are usually the other fellow's.

Newspaper Editorials.—The easiest exercise on discovering fallacies may be had with newspaper editorials. These are often written to be consistent with a known attitude or policy in regard to public questions. Some newspapers have a consistent prejudice against England or Japan, against the Republican party or the Democratic party, against the League of Nations, or they may be consistently conservative, liberal or radical. Special pleaders seek to justify themselves, not necessarily to discover the truth. That is the trouble with consistency or dogma. It does not allow one to change one's mind, to face squarely and with easy conscience changing conditions or important additions to knowledge that may demand amendment to preconceived opinions. We believe those things we wish to be true and we read what confirms our beliefs. Read the papers and the editorials opposed to your views and try to find the fallacies in their reasoning.

Informal, good-natured discussion is excellent for clarifying and testing one's opinions. Formal debate is even better for compelling a close scrutiny of the other side. Controversy, when it is not acrimonious, makes the mind more elastic, and is fine practice in quick and accurate thinking.

Saving Time.—One of the chief problems in study is to learn to economize time. Obviously, one should not spend as much time upon a detective story as upon a classic novel. Nobody has put this thought more compactly or completely than Bacon. He says:

Some books are to be tasted, others to be swallowed, and some few to be chewed and digested: that is, some books are to be read only in parts; others to be read but cursorily, and some few to be read wholly, and with diligence and attention.

Skill, then, in the use of books is a prime factor in education, and surprisingly rare. Boswell was astonished at the way Johnson "tore the heart out of a book." Others have been born with the art, or have acquired it, of reading the most in the shortest time. Lyman Abbott in "Silhouettes of My Contemporaries" has this to say of Henry Ward Beecher:

As a student he had extraordinary facility in the use of books. "One does not read a book through," he once said to me. "You read a book as you eat a fish; cut off the tail, cut off the head, cut off the fins, take out the backbone, and there is a little meat left which you eat because it nourishes you." . . . I took over to him one day a new volume in philosophy. . . . I wanted to get his estimate upon it. He took the book with him to the dinner table and read while he ate, turning over the leaves with remarks such as: "Nonsense! Of course . . . Everybody knows that . . . Borrowed from Spurzheim . . . That's new and well worth thinking about!" At the end of the meal he had finished the book and handed it back to me with a ten-minute comment which made the basis of my editorial review.

Skilful Selection.—Psychologists have been recently experimenting with students in order to find out something practical about the rate of speed in reading. Interesting comparisons can no doubt be made to show how much faster than others some read a given passage and express accurately the content, but it is doubtful whether any method or device can help the individual more than the usual practice and experience. Expert readers are those who show common sense in the matter of experience. If they are looking for specific facts they take the short cuts to the information. They are not like so many young debaters who waste hours in floundering through discouraging masses of material. Efficient reading is often only a matter of examining the table of contents or the index for a clue, of reading the preface for the author's purpose or point of view, of noting the chapter headings, of looking for summaries at the ends of chapters. Opening or closing sentences of paragraphs often contain the gist of the matter. Training the eye in looking for key nouns and verbs as one glances down the page is helpful. Even good books contain much material irrelevant to the purpose of the reader and many are padded with material that is of interest to but few. Other chapters are useful, but the student has perhaps read fully on the subject in other books.

Accuracy.—In this business of stripping a book, the reader must not, of course, overlook its kernel. He must make haste carefully. All this strategy is preliminary to the study which must be unhurried and concentrated. No indifferent dawdling or cramming will serve here. Ruskin is our most eloquent preacher on this text. Listen to him:

First of all I tell you earnestly and authoritatively (I *know* I am right in this) you must get into the habit of looking intensely at words, and assuring yourself of their meaning, syllable by syllable—nay, letter by letter.

If you read ten pages of a good book letter by letter, that is to say, with real accuracy, you are forevermore, in some measure, an educated person. The entire difference between education and non-education (as regards the merely intellectual part of it) consists in this accuracy.

And this is just what the schools and colleges are apparently not able to teach. They are too crowded to search the individual mind sufficiently. Time and teachers are not available. Garfield's ideal education, "Mark Hopkins on one end of a log and I on the other," is no mere flourish of enthusiasm for the Williams professor.

Reading Not Enough.—Books alone will not make the trained thinker and speaker. Even if the student does not need the interpretation given by another's voice, he may be steeped too much in books. He must have considerable contact with men and affairs if he would have confidence, fluency, and precision of speech. Here again Bacon's sententious wisdom is enlightening: "Reading maketh a full man, conference (conversation) a ready man, and writing an exact man."

Conversation.—Conversation is not generally thought of as educational. It implies idle chatter, or, at best, recreation. And yet that earnest scholar and man of the world, Mahaffy, writes:

Many men and many women owe the whole of a great success in life to this and nothing else . . .

And though men are supposed to succeed in life by dead knowledge, or by acquaintance with business, it is often by their social qualities, by their agreeable way of putting things, and not by their more ponderous merits that they prevail.

Conversation gives us opportunity to test the ideas gained from books. It is often humiliating but salutary to try to tell or explain our thought. We find it is vague or confused or incomplete. Making it clear to another clarifies it for us. "Teaching teaches teachers." Better still if the listener disagrees. He compels us to bring forth illustrations, analogies, proof, colorful and forceful speech. Benjamin Franklin, in his "Autobiography," speaks of the valuable training he got in his conversation with his young friend Collins. They used to walk in the woods on Sundays and talk for hours of their reading and their opinions on current events. They disagreed on their most interesting topics and so had delightful tussles which exhilarated both their minds and bodies. Many college students have testified to getting more of permanent value in conversation with their instructors or their fellow-students about their work than in the formal courses of study. This was indeed the method of the ancient Greeks. Socrates, the father of dialectics, questioned his small group of pupils, made them confess their lack of logic, and in informal discussion led them to sound thinking. The great Teacher exalted conversation as education. Jesus trained his ignorant fishermen and artisans to direct the greatest educational movement in history.

Leaders in modern history have given eloquent testimony to the value of conversation with all classes of people. Gladstone, Palmerston, Fox, Patrick Henry, Clay, Lincoln were always practical and had a cosmopolitan interest in men and women. They learned from the farmer, the laborer, the storekeeper, from the traveler, the diplomat and the scientist. Webster said, "Converse, converse, CONVERSE, with living men, face to face, mind to mind—that is one of the best sources of knowledge."

Lloyd George is often referred to as a man who keeps abreast of the world's thought not only in politics, but in science, philosophy, and art, through his skill in conversation. He has naturally little time for reading, and no doubt is alert to make up for it in talk with the many exceptionally well-informed men that he meets. This does not mean that he is often a silent sponge. He in turn speaks interestingly and instructively out of his vast experience, and so the benefits are mutual. Lloyd George is probably the best debater in England and his close attention to conversation is largely responsible for this talent.

"Talking Shop."—Although talking business at lunch is often condemned, it is much more stimulating and beneficial than the trivial chatter that usually takes its place. We all talk "shop" because it is most interesting to us. No group is much superior to any other in this respect. The "shop talk" of the actor, the professor, the student, the business man may be equally informing and inspiring, or profitless and dull. It is all a matter of the persons conversing. If they refrain from heated or long-winded argument, if they are good-humored, spontaneous, and yet considerate of each one's desire to be heard, wit, philosophy, and sound business sense and often specific suggestions of immediate cash value may result. Many a congenial party makes the lunch hour yield splendid returns in recreation and business.

That fine talker, Robert Louis Stevenson, did not exaggerate the value of conversation, in these words:

> The first duty of a man is to speak; that is his chief business in the world; and talk, which is the harmonious speech of two or more, is by far the most accessible of pleasures. It costs nothing; it is all profit; it completes our education; it founds and fosters our friendships; and it is by talk alone that we learn our period and ourselves.

Exercise 3[1]

The past two centuries have witnessed a complete change in the attitude toward the human factor in industry. Before the development of machinery, human labor was the most important factor in all productive effort. Man's place in the industrial system was taken for granted, and since there was no substitute for human labor in production, attention was concentrated upon the development and utilization of that factor. The introduction of machinery and the development of the factory system brought about a complete change of emphasis. Perfection of machinery became the objective of the period, and the entire battery of scientific research was for the time being trained upon it. New inventions in the field of engineering, significant discoveries along chemical lines, and wonderful accomplishments in the

[1] ROBINSON, WEBSTER, "Fundamentals of Business Organization," p. 76 *ff.*, McGraw-Hill Book Company, Inc.

improvement of industrial technique gave a tremendous impetus to this work of scientific research and to the utilization of its discoveries in industry. Each new advance forced the human factor farther into the background. There developed, as a result, a conspicuous lack of balance between the skill of the worker and the complexity of the machine, which finally forced a gradual reorganization. But this reorganization was little more than a negative move, since its basic idea was merely to simplify the mechanical devices so that they could be profitably utilized. Their adaptation to the physical and mental characteristics of the worker was given no more consideration than was essential to that purpose. The machine was still the center of interest; the controlling element of human ability remained in the background and was but unwillingly recognized.

But a change gradually took place as monopolies were destroyed through the expiration of basic patents, and as markets began to overlap and become highly competitive. This change manifested itself in the attempt to reduce costs and to improve efficiency through other than purely mechanical means. The first attack was made upon the wholly disorganized character of industry. Concentration of all scientific attention upon machinery alone, to the almost total neglect of methods and organization of work, had resulted in extremely low operating efficiency. Taylor, Gantt, Emerson, and other early exponents of scientific organization and management, attributed this condition to the absolute lack of system in operation. They made the first positive move toward remedying the situation by introducing the scientific method into industry. Scientific direction and supervision effected tremendous savings in time, materials, and labor. Effort was directed mainly toward the discovery of the best methods; the workers who were to use these methods were still considered only as a means to an end.

When the World War came, the demands for increased production which accompanied it brought about the development of a new and general feeling of unbalance. For the first time it became very evident that highly developed technique of production, scientifically determined processes, and complicated equipment and machinery were useless without the motivating force of human brain and muscle concentrated in equally efficient and carefully chosen individuals. The conception became widespread that the worker was an end in himself, that his personal welfare and development were of equal or of even greater importance than the products of his labor (greater, because without an efficient worker satisfactory production was impossible). As a result significant changes took place in the industrial field. The most outstanding development was the attempt to secure a closer correlation between the ability of the individual and the work which he was performing; that is, the attempt to fit every man, whether executive or operator, to his job in the organization. But before this could be done the business had to be more or less functionalized, since it is only through functionalization that the various types of jobs can be definitely segregated. Furthermore, it is only with the comparatively recent extension of scientific analysis into the realm of human beings that sufficient knowledge has become available in this field to enable intelligent coordination of the man and the job.

The present emphasis upon the human factor in industry is of great significance. It benefits not only industry but also the whole social system, of which those engaged in industrial pursuits form so large and so important a part. The individual who is contented and efficient in his work is the one who contributes the most to society, who makes the most desirable citizen. Although few of the attempts at scientific analysis, of either the human or the non-human elements in industry, have as yet succeeded in securing absolute results, there is no reason, given sufficient time, why physiology, psychology, and the allied human sciences should not work an improvement in the use of man-power approximate to that already secured in the use of inorganic elements. These sciences may yet be numbered among the most effective tools of industry.

Personnel as an Organization Factor.—This discussion makes no attempt at exhaustive treatment of the field of personnel management. Such an attempt would entail a critical analysis and evaluation of the great mass of data on the subject which has accumulated within recent years. Under the impetus of the war this field was extensively investigated by scientists, personnel specialists, and practical business men. The importance of the personnel problem was established beyond question. Psychologists, physiologists, psycho-pathologists, psychiatrists, industrial engineers, personnel specialists, and business executives, through their studies of the human element in industry and in the army, gathered together a wealth of data which progressive management may draw on for guidance in the task of handling its men. Although in many cases no definite conclusions have been reached and many findings have yet to be established as facts, the work of these men is becoming institutionalized and is constantly gaining a firmer hold in industry. The chief danger is that a false feeling of completion may arise, arresting further progress of the work and making that which has already been accomplished undesirably rigid. The scope of the personnel field is so far-reaching, and the possibilities for the development of organized knowledge concerning it are so great, that it is replete with opportunities for further invention, experimentation, and control. In its present unfinished state, to attempt to criticize or evaluate the accumulated data concerning personnel would be futile. This must be left to the scientists and specialists who have already done such admirable work in the field.

This discussion is considering personnel not as a problem of management, but as an organization factor for which adequate provision must be made before good management is possible. It will therefore take account of the tools of personnel research only so far as they relate to, and clarify, the problem of matching the job and the man. This problem is only one phase of the whole personnel question; but it is undoubtedly the most difficult, and its proper solution the most vital.

Getting the Right Man in the Right Place—A Fundamental of Organization.—In organization analysis, the necessity for matching the man and the job—getting the right man in the right place—is recognized as a fundamental of organization. When there is a given group of functions to be performed and a given group of men to perform them, great care should be exercised in matching each man, as nearly as possible, to the function which he is to carry out. This statement seems axiomatic. Yet experience has shown that this problem rarely receives adequate consideration. The negligence of those in authority may be attributed to any or all of three reasons:

first, they do not know what is meant by matching the man and the job; second, they fail to appreciate its necessity; third, they do not know how to do it. The purpose of this discussion is to analyze, in so far as limited space and the present development of technique will permit, these phases of the third fundamental of organization. Getting the right man in the right place, as a fundamental of organization, is practically incontestable—the only question concerns the tools and the methods to be used in its accomplishment.

Individual and Job Differences.—There are innumerable differences in people, and an almost equal variation in the character of jobs. Unless these differences and variations are taken into consideration in placing men, business will neither secure the full value of the abilities of its executives and workers, nor allow the individuals to use them to their own best advantage. Considering the matter from a purely practical standpoint, the study of these differences in people and the differences in jobs is the only method which will enable managers to find men who can actually do the work and successfully fill the positions in their organizations.

Individual Differences.—Individuals differ widely. It is unusual to find two men who, even in appearance, resemble each other to a marked degree; and it is still more exceptional to find two who react in the same manner under identical circumstances. Variations in appearance and action, however, are but outer and easily seen differences in fundamental qualities. Scientists have proved that men are, from birth, unequal in mental and physical capacities—that even the possibility of developing particular capacities varies to a remarkable extent in each individual. These inherent or natural differences may be modified or enhanced, but almost never, save in exceptional cases, completely overcome by subsequent training and experience. To determine exactly what these differences between individuals are, and what their consequent effect upon future development and action will be, is the most difficult task in the whole range of personnel work. But this task must be performed if personal abilities and characteristics are to be given intelligent consideration in the organization of a business.

Physical Variations in Individuals.—The major physical variations in individuals are easily detectable. The chief danger in determining these differences is that too great attention will be given to the outstanding physical traits, while the subtler differentiations are overlooked. It is not difficult to decide that a man's strength is below average; neither does it require any lengthy deliberation to determine that his muscular control is defective in certain respects. These are more or less obvious limitations. Differences in height, weight, muscular strength, and general bodily development can be recognized almost immediately, and the degree of their variation from the average, or from the desired standard, determined with but little difficulty.

The consideration of what may be called the general "motor capacity" of individuals reveals further physical diversity in human beings. A man may have unusual strength and yet be unable to utilize that strength except in the performance of the simplest tasks, through lack of precision and control of movement which another man may have to a marked degree. The motions of certain individuals may be characterized by steadiness and deliberation, while those of other persons may be very rapid but equally accurate. The skill of one man may lie in his ability to perform a simple motion with unusual speed, while that of another may consist of being able to secure coordinated action in the performance of several complicated motions. These varying, more or less hidden, characteristics are fully as significant as the more obvious ones.

Still less apparent, and consequently less easily determinable, are the physical differences resulting from variations in the keenness of the sense perceptions. The same food may not have the same flavor to two individuals, simply because the sense of taste may be more highly developed in one than in the other. Range and length of vision, as well as rapidity and keenness of visual perception, are possessed by various individuals in markedly varying degrees. The difference in the amount and accuracy of the visual images which can be recorded by different people in the same length of time is found to be considerable. Although some people are very sensitive to shades of color, color-blindness, especially among men, is a fairly common visual defect. Differences in the sense of touch and in auditory perception are equally great. Certain people, for example, are highly sensitive to tactual impressions, while others find difficulty in distinguishing between various kinds of material without the aid of senses other than touch. Differences in the ability to hear distinctly, and to retain oral impressions, are so common as to need no explanation. The difficulty lies in determining accurately the keenness or the dullness of the auditory perception of any particular individual. All of these factors have a distinct bearing upon the individual's fitness to perform certain types of work within the organization, since each type usually requires the possession of one or more of these senses in a more or less highly developed state.

Mental Differences in Individuals.—Physical variations are no more important than mental ones. The physical and mental characteristics of an individual are so closely connected that an analysis of one without the other is of but uncertain value in fitting the man to the job. A man's mental make-up may have an overwhelming influence upon his capacity to utilize his physical abilities, and his physical make-up may be a help or a hindrance in the fulfillment of his intellectual possibilities.

There are, in general, three phases of mental make-up through which individual differences are manifested—temperament, intellect, and moral character. In temperament and emotional characteristics lie those differences which are commonly referred to as differences in "human nature." Some men are nervous and easily excitable, prone to hasty and thoughtless action; while others are calm and not easily aroused, given to deliberate and meditated procedure. The former might be adversely affected by being compelled to perform monotonous work or to carry on the work in noisy surroundings, while the latter would feel no injurious effects under such circumstances. This is primarily a matter of temperament.

Just as there seems to be an inherent difference in individual temperament, so there is an inherent difference in individual intellectual ability, commonly referred to as intelligence. There is a marked variation in ability to absorb knowledge, to respond to training. There is, moreover, a peculiar characteristic of this variation which is particularly significant in fitting the man to the job. People differ not only in *general* intellectual ability but also, and more widely, in intellectual ability along relatively specialized lines. Even within the same trade, occupation, or business, intellectual variations are noticeable. For example, the man who is a remarkably good accountant might fail utterly in the sales department, simply because his special aptitude did not lie in that direction. In some cases, the spread of intellectual ability is so great, the intellectual balance of the individual so fine, that it is difficult to determine the particular lines along which his intellect functions with greatest keenness. But these cases are not common, and there is usually a determinable tendency toward some one field of activity. This by no means implies that, were every individual placed in the work for which he has been best fitted by his intellectual inheritance, he would immediately accomplish extraordinary results. Geniuses are rare, and their ability is concentrated to an unusual and often undesirable degree upon a single phase of mental activity. It does imply, however, that a person of so-called normal general intelligence, if given proper education and training in the field to which his individual type of intellect is particularly adapted and in which he is most interested, will be more susceptible to this training and will reach a higher level of efficiency as a result of it, than if he were being instructed along some other line. Furthermore, no amount of training can give the "knack" of the work to the person who lacks the fundamental aptitude for it, and he is therefore at a disadvantage when competing with the man who is primarily suited to it. These fundamental differences in intellectual capacity are additional forces contributing to the variation in individual adaptability to the many dissimilar types of activities performed in the business organization.

People differ in still another phase of their mental make-up; that is, in moral character. In the study of this phase, science has made but little progress. Psychologists admit its importance, recognize the influence of direction and training on its development, and grant its existence in varying degrees in different individuals. But they make no claim to ability to ascertain, by any scientific method of measurement, the strength or weakness of a person's moral character. Certain individuals are of unquestionable honesty and integrity; others are honest and reliable only to a degree which suits their own purposes and enables them to evade actual punishment by society; still others cannot be trusted in any circumstances. The problem is to determine in which category an individual should be placed, without the necessity of finding out perhaps by unfortunate experience. The necessity of determining these moral characteristics before employing or placing a man depends, of course, upon the type of work which he is to do. Provided that he is not a criminal, the moral character of a laborer is of comparatively little import. But the honesty and reliability of the bank cashier is a matter of extreme consequence. There is as yet no satisfactory method of determining moral character. It is known only that individuals vary in its possession.

Influence of Education, Training, and Experience.—Education, training, and experience play an important part in developing and fixing personal characteristics. Two men, whose physical endowments were originally almost equal, may vary widely in their ability to perform certain kinds of work involving muscular activity, because one has benefited by physical training which has been denied to the other. Of two men, both with a native intellectual tendency toward mechanics, one may be fitted only for work in a machine shop, while the other, owing to additional advantages of education and training, is capable of designing machinery. Temperamental and moral differences may also be created by education and training.

In almost any field, and particularly in business, people differ owing to the influence of the individuals under whom they have received their training. In selecting men for executive positions, it will often be found that those who have been under the direction of a man with real executive ability will have so thoroughly absorbed his viewpoint that they too are fitted for the higher executive positions. The viewpoint of the men who have been trained by a "detail" executive, however, is liable to be so circumscribed that they are suited only for minor positions in the organization. Investigation has shown that a man's viewpoint in business is almost entirely determined by the training and experience which he has received and by the personal influences to which he has been subject.

Job Differences.—Within industry as a whole, and even within the structure of a single organization, there is a wide range of jobs whose differences are almost as great as those to be found existing among individuals. In practically any business, the variation between the characteristics of the administrative, the executive, and the supervisory positions, and the workers' jobs is so wide that they demand totally different qualities and capacities, while the latter jobs run the whole gamut of differences in the abilities they require. There are three general classes of positions in almost any business; those which require mainly mental effort; those which demand primarily physical exertion; and those which necessitate a combination of both types of activity.

The differences between the jobs included in these categories are best illustrated by citing a few general examples of the individual characteristics, or the types of individuals, which they require. The administrative position at the head of the business has a broader outlook and a wider scope of activity than any other in the organization. It demands, consequently, an especially strong imaginative tendency, the ability to think in large terms and to visualize as a whole not only the nature of the present trend both within and without the business, but also the probable future trend. This position makes almost no demand upon physical or motor capacity, but usually requires, for its attainment, a comparatively long period of training and experience.

This is also largely true of all executive positions which demand, primarily, sound and rapid judgment, the ability to select and lead men, the ability to delegate detail, and sound training in technique. Positions as department heads vary in character and requirements with the type of work being done in the department. The sales manager's job, like that of the head of the business, requires an abundance of imagination; the chief accountant's position necessitates a mechanical turn of mind; while the job as head of the production department calls for technical knowledge of materials, methods, machinery, and general operation. While all of these executive positions demand a certain knowledge of detail, in order that affairs within the department may be efficiently directed and controlled, they also require the ability to subordinate that detail to consideration of the department as a whole; that is, the ability to make detail routine and automatic, so that it will not draw attention from larger problems. Supervisory positions require detailed knowledge of the work being done and constant and intimate contact with it, through the performance of supervision and instruction. These jobs also demand a certain amount of physical ability and skill along with mental requirements.

By far the widest range of variation in requirements is found in that class of jobs concerned with the actual operation of the business, in which the work of the organization is finally executed. At the top of the scale are jobs such as those of the skilled mechanic, the production clerk, the inspector, the draughtsman, and similar operators. In all of these jobs something more than average intelligence and a special aptitude along one line are necessary to supplement a certain amount of physical skill. Requiring less mental ability and more physical dexterity are jobs which involve the sorting or assembling of machine parts, the packing of goods for shipment, and similar activities. As the scale is descended, the amount of mental ability required becomes constantly less, until those jobs such as automatic machine tender or ordinary laborer are reached. These demand almost no mental ability, but largely average physical strength or dexterity. In fact, for automatic machine tending it has been found that individuals even mentally defective are satisfactory and valuable workers, and for extremely monotonous work they are often actually preferable, since the mind of the defective is not subject to the strain which might seriously affect the worker of normal intelligence.

Obstacles to Perfect Coordination of Job Requirements with Personal Qualifications.—The ideal state of affairs within a business would be that in which every position was filled by a man whose physical and mental characteristics were better suited to the position which he occupied than to any other. Under existing conditions, the attainment of such a state is impossible. Neither the material nor the human sciences have progressed far enough in their study of industry to enable accurate determination of the exact qualities and capacities which are required for efficient performance of a particcular job, or of the specific characteristics which are possessed by the individual to make him fit or unfit for the job in question. Even though it were possible to determine these factors with absolute exactitude, there would still be an obstacle to the perfect coordination of personal qualifications with job requirements. The limitations in individual ability, and the limitation in the sources from which men can be drawn to fill the various positions in the organization, make it impossible, in a majority of cases, to find just the type of man desired.

But in the carefully functionalized organization, a majority of the positions have well-defined requirements which remain virtually the same during the operation of the business. Success in placement depends upon the ability to find men who can meet these requirements satisfactorily. The scope of the position itself usually cannot be altered without undesirable disarrangement of the functional structure. Since it is rarely possible to secure the *ideal* man, it is frequently necessary to take the best *available* man. Especially in the case of executive positions, the individual selected will often possess not all, but only the most important qualifications and characteristics essential or desirable. Some provision must consequently be made for supplying those qualities in which he is deficient, or for offsetting those tendencies which are too highly developed. This can best be done by "balancing" the individuals in the organization; that is, by so combining the efforts of two or three that their concerted action will ultimately produce the type of results desired in the position. The executive with a tendency to generalize, for example, should be provided with an assistant who will give proper attention to detail; and the hasty, impetuous executive should be offset by the restraining influence of an assistant whose actions are calm and deliberate. This combination of opposite or complementary temperaments and capacities is possible only when the executive himself recognizes his special ability, and the necessity of balancing or supplementing it by other qualities. The combinations should be made with extreme caution, since not all types of men will cooperate with each other, and harmony is essential to the success of these relations.

Exercise 4[1]

Business forecasts and scientific planning have increased rapidly in importance for a number for reasons, the chief of which are:

1. Predictions and plans based on statistical forecasts have proved of dollars-and-cents value under actual trial. They have served to avoid loss and have allowed correlation of activities through planning to a degree hitherto unknown.

2. The steady growth in size of business concerns has gradually changed the control of activities from a personal basis to a statistical basis. One man no longer governs the destinies of his business, as formerly. He must have lieutenants, and his survey of his business activities must be done through a study of graphs and statistics rather than through his own personal observations.

3. There has been a constant increase in the number of processes which intervene between the raw material and the final sale to the consumer. This has brought about great interrelation between various industries, so that the fortunes of one invariably react in some measure upon another. The approximate effect is often statistically calculable.

4. The lack of balance between supply and demand, most noticeable in the so-called business cycle, and present in practically every business in the form of seasonal fluctuations, has brought attention to the various devices for foretelling such radical changes and making advance preparations.

5. The incessant publicity given to business forecasting has brought about a general interest in its possibilities. The various forecasting services have spent much money in advertising their accomplishments, and business schools have inaugurated courses which teach the principles of statistical prediction.

6. The force of competition is constantly compelling the abandonment of guesswork methods in favor of those founded on facts. Intuitive planning, or even planning based on experience, cannot compete with planning based on facts.

Definition.—Every approach to a scientific problem presupposes definitions. A prediction is a present estimate of circumstances and tendencies as they will exist at a specified

[1] WHITE, PERCIVAL, "Forecasting, Planning, and Budgeting in Business Management." p. 1, *ff.*, McGraw-Hill Book Company, Inc., 1926.

time in the future.   Its value will depend in great measure upon the accuracy and sufficiency of the data upon which it is based.

A scientific prediction is one that, in attempting to lay out the course of a future event, endeavors to take cognizance of all the facts and factors affecting the future of the prediction.

It is essential to understand the relation of prediction to planning.   Prediction is an envisagement of a future result that may be due to a combination of a number of discernible causes, possibly under the control of the predictor and possibly not.   To plan is simply to schedule the measures which it is desired to take with the forces and material available.   Prediction is a guide to planning.

For example, a storm may be predicted within three hours. Nothing can avert the storm or influence it, but the individual can plan to stay indoors, or to carry an umbrella, or to catch some of the rainwater to put in the battery of his automobile. Having the basic prediction of a storm, he can predict what would happen *if* he should go out with an umbrella but no rubbers, *if* he should go out with rubbers and no umbrella, *if* he should stay at home, and any other number of other results *if* he should follow various courses of action.   Taking some secondary prediction as a guide, he can plan to conduct himself and to use his resources so that these factors, coupled with the uncontrollable but predictable factor of the storm, will leave him in the best position.

So also, where the factors of a given causal sequence may be varied at will so as to make various results predictable, as in the case of some factory management problems, that combination is selected which warrants the most desirable prediction, and then the plan is made to realize the combination.   Prediction is a guide to conduct; planning is the scheduling of that conduct.

The architect who designs a railroad terminal must predict, or have someone predict for him, traffic conditions for many years ahead, possible lines of development, and many other things. He predicts the kind of results that he can get from certain materials arranged in certain designs.   Then he plans to bring about the combination of results that give promise of greatest service in the light of the original traffic predictions.

Business Planning and Prediction.—Planning, as has been said, is applied prediction. Almost every business prediction suggests the necessity for a plan. Business planning takes into consideration the past, the present, and the future. While using the prediction, which is based upon statistics, it adds also the human factor of interpretation and judgment. Every great business man has been a great predictor. While in the past his predictions have often been intuitive, in the future, methods of prevision will be those of the laboratory man rather than those of the clairvoyant.

Prediction and planning presuppose a distinction between past, present, and future. This difference can be brought out more clearly by comparing these three states of time with the adjoining territories through which a railroad line runs, traveling from the past, through the present, toward the future. The present is that little region which surrounds the railroad train and which is illuminated by its lights. Beyond, in both directions, there is darkness. The fields which have been passed through are remembered but cannot be seen, while those the train is about to enter show up but dimly ahead.

Hard as it is to peer into the future, it is essential to do so. For this purpose, the locomotive is provided with a headlight which illuminates the rails, and allows the engineer to see any dangers or obstacles ahead. By avoiding accidents, he can drive more safely at a higher speed.

The beams from the headlight illuminate the nearer objects more sharply than those which lie farther off. The brighter and better focused it is, the farther it is possible to see. This implies the need for installing the best headlamp which can be found, computing its projective power most scientifically, fashioning its parabolic surface with the most exacting care, and keeping it always highly burnished. In business, predictions and plans are used as headlights to illuminate the future.

Every business depends in some degree upon prediction. The speculative business, so called, is merely that one which is most difficult to forecast. Ordinarily speaking, the difference between a safe and an unsafe business is largely a matter of ability to predict. In other words, the more predictable a business becomes, the more likely it is to be successful. If the future of a business can be known, it can be provided for, and, therefore, the business becomes safe.

The Bases of Prediction.—Every prediction and every plan are made up of the following components:

1. *Sources.*—These may be statistical compilations, the consensus of many opinions, the tabulation of observations or experiments, or other data worthy of serving as the basis of a prediction and a plan.

2. *Interpretation.*—Statistics alone are not sufficient. They must be interpreted by someone cognizant of the situation and able to correlate the various factors, and to gather their true meaning.

3. *Presentation.*—The methods of presenting the facts statistically, graphically, and personally are of the greatest importance. A prediction report and a written plan are advisable.

4. *Application.*—After the statistics of the past have been gathered, interpreted, and presented, it remains to apply them to practical account in the major fields of purchasing, production, and marketing.

The technique of making predictions and turning them into business plans, carefully correlated with national and industrial plans, is a comparatively new science. Like all similar endeavors it is still in an experimental stage. Yet the mere fact that it is possible to predict in many lines, and the short period of time over which statistics have been kept, show in some degree what may be expected in the future along the lines of scientific planning.

Sources of Prediction.—Predictions are founded upon facts. If these facts are inaccurate, if the number gathered is insufficient, or if the interpretation is faulty, the prediction will be nullified to a great degree.

Only the largest organizations, however, can afford to hire their own staff specialists to collect and to compile all the statistics necessary for purposes of prediction. The smaller concerns, which in many ways are in much greater need of scientific methods of planning, have neither the funds nor the resources to collect many of the necessary facts external to the organization but vital in their effect upon its activities. It will be necessary, therefore, for such concerns either to subscribe to the forecasting services available, or to accept the statistics of the various trade journals and reporting services, and from them to make up their own predictions.

The average concern will, therefore, take its facts from three series of sources:

1. External statistics (those having to do with general business conditions) will be taken in digested form from one of the forecasting services.

2. Industrial statistics (those having to do with the industry of which the company is a member, or perhaps with other industries which are closely related in cause and effect) will be taken from reporting services, such as Dun's, Bradstreet's, trade journals, and similar organizations.

3. Internal statistics (those having to do with the activities of the company itself) will be secured from purchasing, production, sales, and accounting records, or any other sets of company statistics which may prove suitable for purposes of prevision.

Interpretation.—The analysis of statistics prior to drawing up the prediction is one of the most important tasks in making a forecast. The person who makes this forecast must, therefore, possess in high degree the ability to correlate the various facts without bias and with due regard to the proper weight to ascribe to each. He must also be able to see ahead and take into consideration the various external forces which are at work and which may make the ultimate prediction deviate from its normal procedure.

The person who interprets the statistics should not necessarily make up the primary records. Indeed, the preliminary routine work is usually done by subordinates. But the interpreter should begin his task with the sorting out of the essential facts from the unessential ones.

The ultimate prediction is a resultant of forces. A great deal of its accuracy will depend upon the skill of the interpreter in assigning to each set of facts the weight or force which it will exert in determining the final result. Steps can then be taken to cope with the adverse factors. Indeed, prediction and forecasting have been defined as foresight of consequences and provision against them.

Presentation.—The value of the prediction is greatly lessened unless it is presented to the management in a usable and practicable form. This ordinarily implies graphic analysis, because the average executive has neither the time nor the technical training to digest a mass of statistics. Numerical relationships must be translated into diagrams before they can be judged accurately.

Predictions are usually submitted in the form of reports. The construction and the wording of these reports should be of the simplest, so that they may be readily understood by everyone concerned.

It is often of the greatest importance to have predictions and conclusions explained personally to the heads of the business. The forecaster should be able to participate in the discussions, and to show how he has arrived at his results.

Application.—The gathering of statistics and the making of predictions are practically useless unless they are to be put to work in the making of plans. The first place where they prove of utility is in the layout of long-range policies. Each company wants to look ahead for a number of years so that it can provide for expansion and development of the business. It often happens, for example, that a manufacturer can see ahead to the time when he will have filled the demand for his product through present channels. If he is to continue expanding his business, he must find new uses for the product or provide new markets before the saturation point in the original market has been reached. Through correlation of statistics, he knows approximately what his present market is and how long it will be before he has satisfied it. He also knows that he must be prepared for the future increase in output of his factory. In some industries, this question is particularly acute. In the case of rubber, for example, experts are constantly devising new methods of disposing of the output.

Types of Predictions.—Scientific prediction falls into two main classes:

1. Predictions of effects in which the predictor can control the causes.

2. Predictions in which the predictor can observe but is powerless to control the result.

The first class of prediction is that of scientific method, pure and simple. For example, by laboratory tests it is proved that a drill of a certain standard specification will go through a steel plate of known grade and thickness in 30 seconds if operated at the rate of 200 revolutions a minute. The test has been made on a great number of plates, a table of results has been drawn up, and all errors corrected. As far as tools and machinery are concerned, the shop foreman can be told that two plates a minute should be punctured.

At this point, however, the second type of prediction enters, because it is not possible to predict with scientific accuracy how fast the individual operator of the machine will work. The prediction can be made, but it will now be based on statistics and averages of various sorts, and predictions will be more and more accurate as the number of operators involved increases. The second method, therefore, must be used where an essential factor cannot be controlled.

Life insurance is an excellent example of prediction where probabilities and chances are accounted for. Like the causes of variation in individual character, the causes of death at various ages are almost endless. Nevertheless, if enough cases of death are enumerated, a table can be constructed to show for each age what the predictable number of remaining years of life will be. This is known as a mortality table. By its use, insurance companies know how much money to charge as a premium during a period of years to enable them to pay death benefits when death does occur. Actuarial science has a low margin of error, even though based entirely on observation.

Business Plans.—Both types of predictions are used in the formation of business plans. The application of forecasting to the financial management of the company's affairs is particularly important. More and more attention is being paid to the question of budgets and budgetary control—a matter which lies almost entirely in the field of prediction.

Applied predictions, or plans, are also of the greatest value in purchasing, production, and marketing. By careful analysis of statistics and by correlation with the general trend of business, it is possible for the purchasing agent of a manufacturing concern, or the buyer for a retail store, not only to regulate his purchases according to size, but also to predict with a fair degree of certainty the price he should pay.

In the field of production, prediction is used to correlate volume of production with the volume of finished article which can be sold. Periods of over- and under-production are being reduced by the use of prevision based on facts. Time and motion studies, scheduling, estimating, and a variety of other special phases of prediction, are also used in production.

The analysis of markets, the setting of sales quotas, the formation of advertising budgets according to planned sales are also matters pertaining to prediction.

From the point of view of forecasting, purchasing, production, and sales are all part of the same process and should be carefully correlated so that activity in one department will be accompanied by activity in another, and so that advance preparations for increased production will be attended by adequate purchases and a suitable sales campaign. Since selling is the final and controlling process, the other two steps should be regulated by the planned volume of sales, and also by the seasonal fluctuation in sales.

The first step in studying practical prediction is an understanding of the various factors involved in making a forecast. These are treated in the following chapter.

FACTORS IN FORECASTING

The factors entering into predictions or plans can be roughly divided into two classifications: first, those which are foreseeable and which, therefore, can be insured against; second, those which are unforeseeable. No exact boundary line can be established between the foreseeable and the unforeseeable, since, as knowledge increases and as records accumulate, there is a tendency for factors originally placed in the latter class to move into the first.

A second group of factors is concerned with the manner of occurrence. The time at which an event will occur, or at which a plan will be fulfilled, is important because of the difficulty of seeing far ahead. The regularity of occurrence will have much to do in determining the distance which can be seen ahead. The number of factors which concur to bring about a certain event are also of great importance, because the more there are of them, the greater difficulty is experienced in planning with accuracy.

A final group of factors is concerned with the interpretation of the statistical components into the finished plan. Here the personal element of judgment plays a leading rôle, and the ability to interpret accurately according to the facts without influence or bias.

Foreseeable Factors.—Foreseeable factors are those which it is in the power of the individual to control, or which he can insure against because of his knowledge of the frequency of their occurrence. These events may occur naturally, or may be set in motion through some human agency.

In the case of accidents in factories, fires in buildings, and other such occurrences, it is usually possible to predict the frequency of occurrence in industry at large, and even to classify the causes of them numerically. That is, so many painters will die of lead poisoning; so many miners will die through explosions in mines; so many railroad employees will be killed, and the like. Although the individual accident cannot be pointed out, yet the general prediction may be made. This has allowed the formation of employers' liability insurance companies, the success of which is founded on the accurate prevision of the elements of risk in different businesses.

It is the object of every business to obtain the utmost possible control over all the conditions surrounding it. Accordingly, the growth of a progressive concern shows a steady conversion of unforeseeable factors into the class of foreseeable factors. For example, a manufacturing concern starts by selling all its goods through a commission house, and has virtually nothing to say about retail distribution. But it finds it cannot make its plans with any accuracy under such conditions, and, consequently, it gradually assumes the function of retail distribution itself.

Although the successful business shows a gain in control, yet it must always reckon with the possibility of some elements falling back again into the class of unforeseeable factors. A well-organized and law-abiding group of workmen may, within a week, become a band of law-breaking strikers, thereby upsetting every arrangement upon which the firm had banked. It is such emergencies which are the hardest to provide for in any business prediction or plan. The predictor can take care of the external and even the entirely uncontrollable matters by insurance, or he can otherwise protect himself against catastrophes. But it is those matters which are on the border line between the foreseeable and the unforeseeable which present the greatest element of uncertainty.

Unforeseeable Factors.—The first class of those indeterminate factors which upset the equilibrium of events consists of influences beyond the control of human action. No one, for instance, can as yet predict the spot where the lightning will strike. A farmer may have every reason to expect large profits from the crops stored in his barn, but this sudden bolt may in one moment annihilate his prospects. Earthquakes, hurricanes, and floods may be classed in the category of those continually recurring phenomena which cannot be foreseen.

"Foreseen," of course, is a word which is constantly shifting in application. Ten years from now, factors which appeared totally unpredictable may be brought within the range of accurate prediction.

The business man may, by insurance or by some other means, shift the element of risk; but this in no manner does away with the risk itself, nor does it bring it any more under his control. He merely pays money to shift the responsibility. That is, he takes on a small but immediate burden in order to avoid shouldering a far greater burden if a certain remote but possible event should take place.

It is the unforeseeable events which most completely nullify predictions. A company may have every prospect of success until some revolutionary invention, protected by patent, develops its prospects almost over night. There are other examples. Infidelity of a trusted employee may seriously inconvenience a business. The bankruptcy of some large customer or creditor may bring on a financial crisis. Well-managed companies recognize that the risk exists and accordingly accumulate reserve funds to guard against sudden and unlooked-for disaster.

Time.—Time is invariably a factor in every problem of business planning. Generally speaking, the more immediate events are easier to predict in detail, while so many intermediate events are interposed between those which are remote that it is much more difficult to give a detailed prognosis, but much easier to make a general prediction. The exceptions to this statement are mostly astronomical, where the laws are sufficiently well known to permit of accurate prediction far ahead of the actual occurrence.

When the occurrence of an event is to take place at some distance in the future, factors once negligible may grow to much greater proportions. It is possible to give to each factor only the weight which it appears to possess at the time. Long-range weather forecasting, for example, is as yet in the embryo stage. Weather forecasts for the ensuing 24 hours are all that the weather bureau cares to be judged upon, although it does attempt to forecast the weather for a week. But there are so many small exceptions unnoticed at the time, which may develop in importance, that the results, even for the shorter period, are often inaccurate.

In certain conditions, the element of time is controlling, as in the case of seasonal depressions. Under certain other conditions, the will of a single individual or group of individuals may delay or precipitate an event. The failure of a business, for example, may be delayed by the efforts of one individual to defer the inevitable moment.

As a rule, general tendencies are much easier to predict than particular events; and the more remote the period to which the prediction applies, the more forcibly is this rule in operation. It is like the observer on a vessel approaching a harbor, who makes out the city as a whole before he can distinguish individual buildings.

PART IV

HOW TO SKIM

READING AND SKIMMING TESTS WITH CURRENT PERIODICALS

Test your speed and accuracy from time to time by measuring yourself as you read or skim articles in periodicals.

Distinguish carefully your *purposes*.

If you wish merely to find out what an article discusses, and cannot learn this from the headline or opening paragraph, remember that you ought to be able to do it fairly well at the rate of *at least* 600 words per minute.

If you seek the main facts and arguments of an article, over and above its subject, you ought to skim over 400 words per minute. Here the rate will vary according to the character of the subject.

Keep in mind that it is much harder to skim through ten articles of 1,000 words each than through one article of 10,000 words. Each change of subject compels you to readjust mentally, to work with a fresh set of meanings, hence to warm up to the job.

Keep in mind, too, that familiar topics may be skimmed far faster than strange ones. To the latter you bring fewer word habits. You must think as you read, and that is hard.

SKIMMING NEWSPAPERS

Skimming a newspaper ought not to require more than fifteen to twenty minutes. Professional men usually devote about this time to the task.

146

You know, of course, that a newspaper is specially organized to make skimming easy. And it would be a fine thing if many other publications would imitate this excellent example.

Read headlines only, at first. And read them at the rate of six words per second or faster.

On a standard newspaper page there may be 400 words or more in all the headlines. Roughly then, you ought to read these in 70 or 80 seconds. With considerable practice and better than average skill, you can double or even treble this rate.

Unless you are reading merely for relaxation, never toil through the full report of a news item which has no practical bearing on your business, or your personal affairs. Read the first few opening lines. They will contain the gist of the event. And that is all you need.

Exercises in Skimming

The purpose of the following exercises is to drill you in catching the essentials of a passage which you lack the time to read straight through.

To get the best results, you ought to have somebody help you by regulating your reading time.

Place a cardboard over the exercise you are about to do. Let your helper have a watch ready, to count seconds.

At the top of each page is indicated the time you are to have for skimming the passage hidden under the cardboard.

When he removes the cardboard, do not try to read the passage line by line; for this will be impossible. Try rather to run your eye down through it, spotting what strikes you as important.

At the end of the allotted time, your helper will replace the cardboard over the passage.

You are then to write down (or dictate) the essential facts you noticed in the passage.

Afterward, compare your report with the passage.

I

(Time allowed is 5 seconds)

Most of this book is devoted to tests which, if carefully done, will improve your reading ability. But if passed over lightly, they will benefit nobody, you least of all. For you will only be wasting such time as you may devote to them, and you may form the notion that they have little utility.

II

(Time allowed is 5 seconds)

Only a child thinks that we read with our eyes alone. Reading is a kind of giving and receiving. We bring to the marks we perceive on the page various subtle mental reactions. Some of these are memories, some thoughts, some emotions. The significance we read into the marks depends, not alone upon these mental responses within ourselves but also upon the entire context of the passage read.

III

(Time allowed is 5 seconds)

Colleges waste time and money whenever they train a student having no mathematical ability to be an engineer. They ruin a young man's future happiness whenever they allow him to spend four years of his life mastering foreign languages which he can never put to any use. Society will in time come to insist that education shall all be founded on two inflexible policies: fitting the man to the job, and fitting the job to the world in which the man is going to live.

IV

(Time allowed is 10 seconds)

Herbert Hoover's project to forestall grave business depressions and panics by holding in reserve a sizable fraction of national and state appropriations for large public improvements is one which the leaders of organized labor as well as several distinguished economists have long advocated. No rational criticism of the idea has ever been advanced; and, as there is every reason of prudence to adopt it, we may expect to see it realized. Within a few years America's economic system will become the stablest ever known. And along with its stability will probably, though not certainly, come a steady growth in volume. For where men feel safe, they dare much. Trade expansion will normally increase if traders know that, even at the worst, they will neither cause nor suffer from a widespread collapse.

V

(Time allowed is 10 seconds)

Why does this country not advance more rapidly in its manufacturing? Because consumers cannot buy as fast as factories can make goods for them. Why cannot the consumers keep up with factories? They cannot, in the first place, because our manufacturers and distributors do not pay back to workers and stockholders enough money; and, in the second place, because most consumers have to save part of their earnings and therefore cannot spend for consumption goods even all of that inadequate total which they receive in the form of wages, salaries and dividends.

Money must flow evenly from producer to consumer and back from consumer to producer again, if we are to maintain steady progress in the expansion of our industrial system.

VI

(Time allowed is 10 seconds)

Business men, bankers, and economists disagree profoundly over the wisdom of extending instalment sales further. Every imaginable opinion has been advanced, and the confusion remains profound. Some would-be specialists allege that instalment selling has revolutionized modern life, while others stoutly maintain that it is bringing us to the brink of disaster. E. R. A. Seligman has collected and classified sixty-seven opinions. He finds that they have been based essentially on the success or failure with which instalment selling has been practised by the witness or else by his competitors in the same business. They do not reflect any sound economic judgment, inasmuch as a method that succeeds in one field may fail in another, as a result of special circumstances.

VII

(Time allowed is 15 seconds)

There has lately been placed on the market a new balanced aluminum alloy whose composition differs strikingly from that of any other commercial product. It is reported to combine lightness and strength more successfully than any of its many predecessors.

Other aluminum alloys generally contain manganese, copper, silicon or magnesium. This one uses only nickel and chromium. Of such heavy ingredients there is barely two per cent.

The new alloy does not tarnish. It does not rust. It is easy to weld. It resists most chemicals. And it fatigues slowly. The serious effects which salt water has upon aluminum in most forms are barely discernible.

Like all other aluminum alloys, this one owes its strength chiefly to the amount of hard rolling or cold working which

It receives while being manufactured. At present it is being produced in four grades representing varing amounts of such treatment.

VIII[1]
(Time allowed is 20 seconds)[1]

The weekly weather report issued yesterday by the government was as follows:

"With moderate temperatures or mild open weather prevailing, husking of corn made good advance during the week in eastern and southern portions of belt. In the northwest portion, particularly in Iowa and parts of South Dakota, wet soft fields and more or less rain delayed husking considerably; in the former states fields were mostly too wet for husking machines and considerable damage to down corn has resulted from dampness. In the more eastern states and in the south conditions were generally favorable.

"While some eastern sections of winter-wheat belt reported rather slow growth because of prevailing coolness, the wheat crop generally made good progress during the week in principal producing sections. The soil continued in good to excellent condition in most districts, especially in normally dry more western portions. In Kansas, wheat is nearly all up and much covers the ground in the eastern counties, while further south excellent progress was made in seeding and the early sown is making good advance. In the more northwestern states rains were of great benefit, with the drought relieved in most heretofore dry areas. In Atlantic Coast States, conditions continued generally favorable, with fall-sown grains making good advance."

[1] New York *Times.*

IX[1]

(Time allowed is 35 seconds)

A REMARKABLE CITY BLOCK

In the midst of New York City stands a building of unique record. It is, first of all, the oldest office building occupying an entire block. When its cornerstone was laid seventy-five years and some months ago it was far uptown. The Legislature in 1852 passed a special act authorizing the purchase of this block, described as "the ground bounded by Third Ave., "Fourth Ave., 9th Street and (on the south) "Stuyvesant St. "and Astor Place," and the holding or conveying the buildings that may be erected thereon. This enabling act was passed for the benefit of the American Bible Society, which from that year has carried on its great work there. The skyscraper had not yet come, for it was only in that year that the first power elevator was installed. Telegraph poles stood on Broadway and street cars were so much disliked by the stage drivers that they purposely drove across the tracks. There were then twenty daily papers, with a combined circulation above 200,000 copies and "a yearly value that must exceed a half million dollars."

No newspaper could then have had a printing plant comparable with that which was housed in the "Bible House." In the seventy-five years since, over 76,000,000 copies of the Scriptures have been printed there. No other printing house has such a polyglot output. Here most of the translating of the Bible into foreign languages has been done, as well as making the American Standard Revised Version of the New Testament. And from this red-brick building, still holding the whole of this site against the tide of tall buildings that have swept by it in this half century of the elevator and the steel beam, the sacred pages of its printing have been carried by train and ship, by wagon and pack animals, by colporteurs and missionaries, to every land on the face of the earth.

Just as a business alone it is one of New York's foremost houses; but when the world-uses to which the vast product is put are considered, it is a business to which New York should be proud to devote a whole block.

[1] New York *Times*.

X[1]

(Time allowed is 55 seconds)

With the largest number of employes of any single business concern in the city, outnumbering the combined Police, Fire and Street Cleaning departments by 9,000, an army of 41,000 New York Telephone Company employes stands by on twenty-four-hour duty to render constant service to the hundreds of thousands of telephones in the city.

The magnitude of the organization and plant necessary to provide telephone service for New York City is displayed by figures furnished yesterday by J. S. McCulloh, president of the New York Telephone Company, showing that in several important respects the telephone service for the five boroughs is the largest single enterprise in the metropolis.

"The figures and comparisons which follow," Mr. McCulloh says, "are interesting as suggesting the natural relationship between the telephone and the economic life of the city. As the world's financial and commercial capital, New York City is necessarily the most highly developed telephone centre. Both because of its size and the character of its activities, it presents extraordinary problems of telephone plant extension, operation and administration."

The 41,000 employes of the company in the city are about three-fourths of the total number employed by the company in its entire operating area, the State of New York. The largest group of employes is the operating force, numbering more than 17,600. There are 2,275 men and women, of whom 1,365 are operators and 237 plant men, on regular night duty at present, the latter to make repairs and to test the equipment for the next day's service.

The maintenance of a skilled operating force requires ten traffic employment offices in the city, the selections of between 9,000 and 10,000 young women employes a year and 190 instructors for training work in the traffic department schools.

In the five years up to 1928, gross additions to plant and equipment in New York City have averaged an actual annual

[1] New York *Times*.

cost of $49,238,400 and net additions have averaged $38,933,200 in the same period. The company occupies 6,619,412 square feet of floor space in 139 buildings, of which it owns eighty-seven, specially constructed for telephone purposes.

More than 8,000,000 miles of wire form the city's network of communication, measuring 325 times the distance around the world, or thirty-four times the distance between the earth and the moon. In the first nine months of the present year alone, 386,000 miles of wire were added to this system. Trunk lines and cables pass through 1,149 miles of telephone subway, containing 6,474 miles of duct.

The total number of telephones in the city, not including private lines, is 1,678,664, or nearly 9 per cent of the 18,893,000 telephones in the United States.

An average of ninety calls a second, or an average of 7,757,511 a day, originate in the city's telephones. This is nearly 70 per cent more than the average daily traffic of the entire state and more than 10 per cent of the total for the entire country. The actual traffic is greater, because thousands of calls enter daily from outside points in this country and from foreign lands.

The unprecedented financial and business activity of recent months has been reflected in heavily increased telephone traffic throughout the city, particularly in the Wall Street district. The largest traffic handled by a single office, as far as records for the year to date indicate, is the Hanover exchange. In a single day 199,636 calls passed through that office, and in a single hour 32,184.

XI[1]

(Time allowed is 5 minutes)

ADDRESS BY CHARLES EVANS HUGHES BEFORE THE BAR ASSOCIATION

"When the three Bar Associations of this judicial department appeared before the Appellate Division petitioning for an investigation of abuses, especially of those connected with what is known as 'ambulance chasing,' we began a new chapter

[1] New York *Times*.

in the history of our bar. We sounded the note of cooperation not simply of lawyers, but of associations of lawyers, thus mobilizing the organized forces of the bar for a definite campaign. We are awakening to the value of this sort of cooperation. What are its objects? What are its difficulties? What should be its methods?

"We wish the entire bar to have a voice, a commanding voice. We desire the concentration of influence. The object is plain enough when there is corruption, when lawyers betray their clients or are false to their larger trust, perverting the machinery of the courts to make it a vehicle of fraud and a device to ensnare the unfortunate. Then, the outraged sentiment of the entire bar should find expression in investigation, condemnation and redress. It should clean its own house. It should demand of the courts the purging of their administration. The way to proceed has been shown in the recent inquiries. By our united action the latent powers of the court were called into exercise, the expert service of lawyers was volunteered, and the needed measures of reform both in court rules and legislation have been recommended.

"We need something more than this sort of dealing with plain abuses. We desire to improve the tone of the bar, to stiffen its self-respect, to secure a wider appreciation of professional standards. These are not the arbitrary standards of a caste. To commercialize the bar, to introduce the methods of solicitation, of mass production, of trading on the opportunities for litigation, is inevitably to encourage frauds and perjuries and to destroy the sense of the personal, fiduciary relation which protects both the client and the court. To preserve the sentiment which subordinates gain to the conception of professional duty, which makes reputation for soundness of advice, for integrity in counsel and performance, for loyalty to the client, to the court and to the law, the most highly prized reward in a career of constant toil amid temptations and incitements to laxity—this is the great object which is fostered in our associations and gives zest to our cooperative endeavors.

"With this zeal for the standards of the profession, we are equipped to aid in the never ending task of improving the methods of administration of justice—in the constant pruning to get rid of what is archaic, superfluous and injurious. We need daring and skillful surgery, as well as medicine, and it is a wise conservatism that knows how to employ both.

"The difficulties of cooperation are no less manifest than its needs. The very size of the bar, with its many thousands of members in this great metropolis, is baffling. We have reason to fear that many are coming to the bar who are unfitted to appreciate the requirements of professional duty. We have not only the problems of technical legal education, the special equipment for practice, but the greater difficulties with respect to general culture and ethical training. But this is by no means the worst phase. The example of lawyers who succeed, either despite or by help of their misdeeds, causes the diseases of the administration of justice to spread like an epidemic. Well-meaning young practitioners are corrupted by their elders who thrive on dishonorable and unprofessional practices.

"Our trouble is not simply in keeping the pestilence out of the temple, but in destroying it inside. How are we to do this, with these vast thousands of practitioners in a community where disregard of law is flaunted on every side? I believe that never at any place or never at any time has it been more difficult to maintain the standards of justice than here and now. We are grateful for the contagion of health, that the leaven of wholesome professional opinion is at work, but we must appraise the task.

"Another difficulty is in the preoccupations of the better men at the bar. In this community, when a man is found who is well trained, dependable, faithful and wise, as a good lawyer should be, the demands upon him mount to incredible burdens. The better youngsters in our law offices become crowded with work. The burden bearers of middle life are bowed down by the multiplying cares of confiding clients. It is a sad spectacle in one sense to see gifted men so absorbed, but it is also inspiring. Despite the large pecuniary returns of success, what a vast amount of unrequited labor is performed by these men at our bar. Once the cause is espoused by a lawyer worthy of the name no effort is too great. The demands of reputation, the sense of obligation, of honor, gives the urge. Yet these overworked men are the leaven of the bar. It is to them we must look for every cooperative effort that is worthwhile. It is the preoccupation of lawyers rather than their indifference that constitutes our most formidable obstacle.

"Another difficulty which we encounter when we come to deal with certain questions is diversity of interests. This is conspicuous in the selection of judges. Lawyers have not one voice. They are divided by their political affiliations. They wish good men on the bench, but they are responsive to the appeals of party associates and political expendiency. Then when we come to broad questions of changes in the law and procedure we meet different opinions conscientiously maintained. Lawyers are experts in criticism. They are the natural antagonists of paper reforms. They are conservatives by training and they are always ready to turn their batteries of reason on what they think are ill conceived proposals of change.

"There is nothing extraordinary about this. If theologians cannot agree, if scientists dispute, why should lawyers be expected to have a common philosophy or to hold the same views as to reforms in law and administration? When we deal with corruption with crying abuses, we may expect unanimity at least in condemning an offense, if not a particular individual. But when measures of reorganization, of reconstruction of the facilities of justice are proposed, differences in conviction, in political philosophy, in predilections, at once appear and the trained combativeness of lawyers has a fair field.

"It is sometimes said that lawyers largely compose our legislatures and therefore they could reform the law and procedure if they would. But lawyers in respect to legislation have not the unity of a single interest. The difficulty increases with the importance of the subject. It is least in minor matters of procedural reform. It is the greatest when we consider constitutional changes which would alter radically the judicial organization or dispense with historic arrangements which in the past have been deemed so essential to liberty that they have been protected by the great guarantees of the fundamental law.

"In the face of these obstacles, what should be the methods of our cooperation? At once we observe the importance of main·

taining our existing associations which have their roots in local sentiment and to some of which are attached the most precious traditions of service and fraternity. We need every bit of help that we can get from these affinities. We cannot accomplish what we seek without the delightful influences of intimate personal fellowship.

"We need the intensive work of small groups. We cannot have the necessary discussion and planning in great meetings, which encourage the expression of extemporized opinions and foster debate rather than a common effort to find solutions. The committees of our associations furnish this opportunity. I have spoken of the preoccupations of the busy men of the bar. Let me now pay the tribute of affection and admiration to the hundreds of these men who add to their enormous burden of professional work the labors of committees which deal expertly with a great variety of subjects, sifting proposals, earnestly striving to find the better ways of administration in their special lines. In the Associations of the Bar of the City of New York we have nearly 600 at work in these committees.

"Of course some of these committees demand only occasional endeavors. They are established to meet emergencies. With others there is the pressure of unceasing demands, as, for example, in the grievance committee, in the committee on the amendment of the law, in committees dealing with particular courts and in special committees addressing themselves to various urgent problems. This intensive work, culminating in well-considered reports, prepares the way for informing the bar, mobilizing its sentiment and neutralizing such opposition as might otherwise come from mere ignorance or prejudice.

"This is the work that can be done in our separate organizations. But when abuses demand the emphatic protest and remedial action of the bar as a whole or opinions on proposed improvements have crystalized so that we can expect them to be promoted by the profession, we need the cooperation of all our associations to speak with the authority of the entire bar. How shall we achieve this?

"We had not long ago a meeting of the presidents of our bar associations in this city at which the subject was discussed. We decided to recommend the organization of a joint committee, a permanent committee of representatives of the associations, to which could be at once referred any matter in which cooperation was desired. Not that such a committee would usurp authority and assume to act for their associations without their consent but that it would provide a ready instrumentality for contract, for exchanges of views and for making speedy arrangements in order to secure the necessary authority for united action. Such a loose, flexible agency is much better than an attempt at this time to obtain a formal, rigid organization. It will utilize, without offense or injury to any, the means of cooperation at our command. It will help all and affront none. This marks a new development of the greatest promise.

"We need more than the cooperation of lawyers. We must have the cooperation of the bench. The judges should know as well as the lawyers, if not better, not only where the need of improvements lies, but the best means of securing it. Sometimes a very small change will produce a great result. Observe, for example, what has been accomplished through the work of the Special Calendar Committee under the auspices of the Appellate Division in this district and with the aid of that great leader in our cooperative efforts and in improving the administration of justice, the presiding justice of this department, Victor J. Dowling. In that committee, judges and lawyers have focused their wisdom and great experience on the evils of congested calendars. I think that this has been the most useful effort of our day. Then, we have the cooperation both in the first and second departments of the bench and the bar in the ambulance chasing inquiries and in the highly important services of Justices Wasservogel and Faber in conducting these inquiries. There is no important reform that cannot be had in the administration of justice if the bench and the bar cooperate to obtain it.

"We also need the cooperation of the community. I shall not waste time on the repute of lawyers. They never have been popular. But while they are, in general, the object of much public objurgation, they are in particular the trusted advisers, the counselors and fiduciaries of the community upon whose expert judgment and trained talent everyone in trouble calls. Let us not forget that law itself is the vital breath of democracy. Despotism exercises an uncontrolled will. In democracy the power of government is subdued to the principles which have general acceptance, and these principles are embodied in what we call the law. It is the only escape from an unbridled official discretion which is the essence of tyranny. Lawyers should be the expert instruments of democracy and the more complicated its mechanisms, the more elaborate the laws which are the product of democracy's legislative workshops, the more necessary is the service of those who devote their lives to the study and interpretation of the laws.

"But no one should forget that while improvement in the administration of justice is the special responsibility of the bar, because of its knowledge and experience, that improvement is sought for the benefit of the community and not for the benefit of lawyers. High-minded lawyers indeed are disheartened and disgusted by favoritisms, delays and abuses. They feel humiliated by perversions of justice. But lawyers are representatives. The real sufferers from defective administration are the clients— the community itself. Lawyers have everything to give to the community and nothing to fear from its action. If the community, apart from the lawyers, could intelligently reform the administration of justice, the lawyers would have no reason to complain. Unintelligent efforts at improvement would only make matters worse and, even then, the lawyers would suffer the least. They would have even more work to do in the endeavoring to disentangle justice.

"The true point of view is that we are all bound together in society. One member, a trade or profession, cannot say to another member, 'I have no need of thee.' Lawyers should recognize their responsibility not because of any selfish interest at stake, but because they have the knowledge, the experience and the skill which are needed. They have the obligations of their equipment. They should realize that their highest privilege is that of the trained servants of democracy. But let all join in the work. If it is a matter of purging the profession of unworthy members, let the bar attend to it. If it is a question of improving the methods of administration, let the bar aspire not to impose its will on the community, but to be the guide, philosopher and friend of all the people in a common effort for the common good.

"We may congratulate ourselves on what has been achieved. Even with respect to our calendars, there has been a notable improvement. The Supreme Court of the United States, the Court of Appeals of this state, the Appellate Divisions, the Federal Circuit Court of Appeals in this circuit, are up to their work and deal with cases practically as soon as they are ready for submission. The ambulance chasing investigation and the recommendations of the special calendar committee have resulted in reducing our trial calendars in considerable measure.

"The great work of legal aid to those who have meritorious cases or defenses but are without means, is better organized and supported through our Legal Aid Society than ever before. How important that work is—the helping hand of the bar to our neighbor who needs expert assistance.

"But this is only a beginning. Most serious delays exist in our courts of first instance, and in our lower courts. The need of improvements is obvious. There are other systems of solicitation besides ambulance chasing which should be broken up. Our procedure, especially criminal procedure, has too many archaic survivals. In several instances, what was once a guaranty of liberty is now a fetter of justice. The system of jury trials for many cases is dilatory and expensive, and in our great cities mocks the tradition that supports it.

"We should be active and persistent, but not impatient. It is not to be assumed that all needed reforms can be accomplished in our day. Even if we could achieve what we desire, the old conflict of good and evil would remain, and perhaps our very achievements would produce new difficulties I am often reminded of the observation of Santayana that in any specific reform we may succeed but half the time, and in that measure of success we may sow the 'seeds of newer and higher evils to keep the edge of virtue clean.' But we have not to do with such later evils. The absolute within us demands that we deal with these evils now existing and within our ken. Who is my neighbor? The lawyer need not pause for a reply. His first charge, his lasting obligation, concerns the administration of justice, and his

keenest satisfaction should be found in the fellowship and cooperation of those devoted to the task of safeguarding and improving
it."

XII

HINTS TOWARDS AN ESSAY ON CONVERSATION

By Jonathan Swift
(Time allowed is five minutes)

I have observed few obvious subjects to have been so seldom,
or, at least, so slightly handled as this; and, indeed, I know few
so difficult to be treated as it ought, nor yet upon which there
seemeth so much to be said.

Most things, pursued by men for the happiness of public or
private life, our wit or folly have so refined, that they seldom
subsist but in idea; a true friend, a good marriage, a perfect form
of government, with some others require so many ingredients, so
good in their several kinds, and so much niceness in mixing them,
that for some thousands of years men have despaired of reducing
their schemes to perfection.   But, in conversation, it is, or might
be otherwise; for here we are only to avoid a multitude of errors,
which, although a matter of some difficulty, may be in every man's
power, for want of which it remaineth as mere an idea as the
other.   Therefore it seemeth to me, that the truest way to understand conversation, is to know the faults and errors to which it is
subject, and from thence every man to form maxims to himself
whereby it may be regulated, because it requireth few talents to
which most men are not born, or at least may not acquire without
any great genius or study.   For nature hath left every man a
capacity of being agreeable, though not of shining in company;
and there are an hundred men sufficiently qualified for both, who,
be a very few faults, that they might correct in half an hour, are
not so much as tolerable.

I was prompted to write my thoughts upon this subject by
mere indignation, to reflect that so useful and innocent a pleasure,
so fitted for every period and condition of life, and so much in all
men's power, should be so much neglected and abused.

And in this discourse it will be necessary to note those errors that are obvious, as well as others which are seldomer observed, since there are few so obvious, or acknowledged, into which most men, some time or other, are not apt to run.

For instance: Nothing is more generally exploded than the folly of talking too much; yet I rarely remember to have seen five people together, where some one among them hath not been predominant in that kind, to the great constraint and disgust of all the rest. But among such as deal in multitudes of words, none are comparable to the sober deliberate talker, who proceedeth with much thought and caution, maketh his preface, brancheth out into several digressions, findeth a hint that putteth him in mind of another story, which he promiseth to tell you when this is done; cometh back regularly to his subject, cannot readily call to mind some person's name, holding his head, complaineth of his memory; the whole company all this while in suspense; at length says, it is no matter, and so goes on. And, to crown the business, it perhaps proveth at last a story the company hath heard fifty times before; or, at best, some insipid adventure of the relater.

Another general fault in conversation is, that of those who affect to talk of themselves: Some, without any ceremony, will run over the history of their lives; will relate the annals of their diseases, with the several symptoms and circumstances of them; will enumerate the hardships and injustice they have suffered in court, in parliament, in love, or in law. Others are more dexterous, and with great art will lie on the watch to hook in their own praise: They will call a witness to remember they always foretold what would happen in such a case, but none would believe them; they advised such a man from the beginning, and told him the consequences, just as they happened; but he would have his own way. Others make a vanity of telling their faults; they are the strangest men in the world; they cannot dissemble; they own it is a folly; they have lost abundance of advantages by it; but, if you would give them the world, they cannot help it; there is something in their nature that abhors insincerity and constraint; with many other insufferable topics of the same altitude.

Of such mighty importance every man is to himself, and ready to think he is so to others; without once making this easy and obvious reflection, that his affairs can have no more weight with other men, than theirs have with him; and how little that is, he is sensible enough.

Where company hath met, I often have observed two persons discover, by some accident, that they were bred together at the same school or university, after which the rest are condemned to silence, and to listen while these two are refreshing each other's memory with the arch tricks and passages of themselves and their comrades.

I know a great officer of the army, who will sit for some time with a supercilious and impatient silence, full of anger and contempt for those who are talking; at length of a sudden demand audience, decide the matter in a short dogmatical way; then withdraw within himself again, and vouchsafe to talk no more, until his spirits circulate again to the same point.

There are some faults in coversation, which none are so subject to as the men of wit, nor ever so much as when they are with each other. If they have opened their mouths, without endeavouring to say a witty thing, they think it is so many words lost: It is a torment to the hearers, as much as to themselves, to see them upon the rack for invention, and in perpetual constraint, with so little success. They must do something extraordinary, in order to acquit themselves, and answer their character, else the standers-by may be disappointed and be apt to think them only like the rest of mortals. I have known two men of wit industriously brought together, in order to entertain the company, where they have made a very ridiculous figure, and provided all the mirth at their own expense.

I know a man of wit, who is never easy but where he can be allowed to dictate and preside: he neither expecteth to be informed or entertained, but to display his own talents. His business is to be good company, and not good conversation; and therefore, he chooseth to frequent those who are content to listen, and profess themselves his admirers. And indeed, the worst conversation I ever remember to have heard in my life, was that at Will's coffeehouse, where the wits (as they were called) used formerly to assemble; that is to say, five or six men, who had writ plays, or at least prologues, or had share in a miscellany, came thither, and entertained one another with their trifling composures, in so important an air, as if they had been the noblest efforts of human nature, or that the fate of kingdoms depended on them; and they were usually attended with an humble audience of young students from the inns of court, or the universities, who, at due distance, listened to these oracles, and returned home with great contempt for their law and philosophy, their heads filled with trash, under the name of politeness, criticism and *belles lettres.*

By these means the poets, for many years past, were all overrun with pedantry. For, as I take it, the word is not properly used; because pedantry is the too frequent or unseasonable obtruding our own knowledge in common discourse, and placing too great a value upon it; by which definition, men of the court or the army may be as guilty of pedantry as a philosopher or a divine; and, it is the same vice in women, when they are over copious upon the subject of their petticoats, or their fans, or their china. For which reason, although it be a piece of prudence, as well as good manners, to put men upon talking on subjects they are best versed in, yet that is a liberty a wise man could hardly take; because, beside the imputation of pedantry, it is what he would never improve by.

     .   .   .   .   .   .

There are two faults in conversation, which appear very different, yet arise from the same root, and are equally blameable; I mean, an impatience to interrupt others, and the uneasiness of being interrupted ourselves; which whoever will consider, cannot easily run into either of those two errors; because when any man speaketh in company, it is to be supposed he doth it for his hearers' sake, and not his own; so that common discretion will teach us not to force their attention, if they are not willing to lend it; nor on the other side, to interrupt him who is in possession, because that is in the grossest manner to give the preference to our own good sense.

There are some people, whose good manners will not suffer them to interrupt you; but, what is almost as bad, will discover abundance of impatience, and lie upon the watch until you have done, because they have started something in their own thoughts which they long to be delivered of.   Meantime, they are so far from regarding what passes, that their imaginations are wholly turned upon what they have in reserve, for fear it should slip out of their memory; and thus they confine their invention, which might otherwise range over a hundred things full as good, and that might be much more naturally introduced.

There is a sort of rude familiarity, which some people, by practising among their intimates, have introduced into their general conversation, and would have it pass for innocent freedom or humour, which is a dangerous experiment in our northern climate, where all the little decorum and politeness we have are purely forced by art, and are so ready to lapse into barbarity. This, among the Romans, was the raillery of slaves, of which we have many instances in Plautus.   It seemeth to have been introduced among us by Cromwell, who, by preferring the scum of the people, made it a court entertainment, of which I have heard many particulars; and, considering all things were turned upside down, it was reasonable and judicious.   Although it was a piece of policy found out to ridicule a point of honour in the other extreme, when the smallest word misplaced among gentlemen ended in a duel.

There are some men excellent at telling a story, and provided with a plentiful stock of them, which they can draw out upon occasion in all companies; and, considering how low conversation runs now among us, it is not altogether a contemptible talent; however, it is subject to two unavoidable defects; frequent repetition, and being soon exhausted; so that whoever valueth this gift in himself, hath need of a good memory, and ought frequently to shift his company, that he may not discover the weakness of his fund; for those who are thus endowed, have seldom any other revenue, but live upon the main stock.

Great speakers in public, are seldom agreeable in private conversation, whether their faculty be natural, or acquired by practice, and often venturing.   Natural elocution, although it may seem a paradox, usually springeth from a barrenness of invention and of words, by which men who have only one stock of notions upon every subject, and one set of phrases to express them in, they swim upon the superfices, and offer themselves on every occasion; therefore, men of much learning, and who know the compass of a language, are generally the worst talkers on a sudden, until much practice hath inured and emboldened them, because they are confounded with plenty of matter, variety of notions, and of words, which they cannot readily choose, but are perplexed and entangled by too great a choice; which is no disadvantage in private conversation; where, on the other side, the talent of haranguing is, of all others, most insupportable.

Nothing hath spoiled men more for conversation, than the character of being wits, to support which, they never fail of encouraging a number of followers and admirers, who list themselves in their service, wherein they find their accounts on both sides, by pleasing their mutual vanity. This hath given the former such an air of superiority, and made the latter so pragmatical, that neither of them are well to be endured. I say nothing here of the itch of dispute and contradiction, telling of lies, or of those who are troubled with the disease called the wandering of the thoughts, that they are never present in mind at what passeth in discourse, is as unfit for conversation as a madman in Bedlam.

I think I have gone over most of the errors in conversation, that have fallen under my notice or memory, except some that are merely personal, and others too gross to need exploding; such as lewd or profane talk; but I pretend only to treat the errors of conversation in general, and not the several subjects of discourse, which would be infinite. Thus we see how human nature is most debased, by the abuse of that faculty, which is held the great distinction between men and brutes; and how little advantage we make of that which might be the greatest, the most lasting, and the most innocent, as well as useful pleasure of life. In default of which, we are forced to take up with those poor amusements of dress and visiting, or the more pernicious ones of play, drink, and vicious amours, whereby the nobility and gentry of both sexes are entirely corrupted both in body and mind, and have lost all notions of love, honour, friendship, generosity; which, under the name of fopperies, have been for some time laughed out of doors.

This degeneracy of conversation, with the pernicious consequences thereof upon our humours and dispositions, hath been
owing, among other causes, to the custom arisen, for sometime
past, of excluding women from any share in our society, further
than in parties at play, or dancing, or in the pursuit of an amour.
I take the highest period of politeness in England (and it is of the
same date in France) to have been the peaceable part of King
Charles the First's reign; and from what we read of those times,
as well as from the accounts I have formerly met with from some
who lived in that court, the methods then used for raising and
cultivating conversation, were altogether different from ours.
Several ladies, whom, we find celebrated by the poets of that age,
had assemblies at their houses, where persons of the best understanding and of both sexes, met to pass the evenings in discoursing
upon whatever agreeable subjects were occasionally started; and
although we are apt to ridicule the sublime platonic notions they
had, or personated in love and friendship, I conceive their refine-
ments were grounded upon reason, and that a little grain of the
romance is no ill ingredient to preserve and exalt the dignity of
human nature, without which it is apt to degenerate into everything that is sordid, vicious and low.   If there were no other use
in the conversation of ladies, it is sufficient that it would lay a
restraint upon those odious topics of immodesty and indencencies,
into which the rudeness of our northern genius is so apt to fall.
And, therefore, it is observable in those sprightly gentlemen
about the town, who are so very dexterous at entertaining a
vizard mask in the park or the playhouse, that, in the company
of ladies of virtue and honour, they are silent and disconcerted,
and out of their element.

   There are some people who think they sufficiently acquit themselves and entertain their company with relating of facts of no consequence, nor at all out of the road of such common incidents as
happen every day; and this I have observed more frequently
among the Scots than any other nation, who are very careful
not to omit the minutest circumstances of time or place; which
kind of discourse, if it were not a little relieved by the uncouth
terms and phrases, as well as accent and gesture, peculiar to
that country, would be hardly tolerable.   It is not a fault in

company to talk much; but to continue it long is certainly one; for, if the majority of those who are got together be naturally silent or cautious, the conversation will flag, unless it be often renewed by one among them, who can start new subjects, provided he doth not dwell upon them, but leaveth room for answers and replies.

XIII

(Time allowed is 32 seconds)

An exchange for the sale of real estate securities exclusively is soon to be established by the Real Estate Board of New York, according to an announcement by the board yesterday. The proposed bureau will be modeled after the idea of the New York Stock Exchange. It will function along the lines of the Stock and Curb Exchanges and will occupy the same relative position in real estate finance as those institutions do in the financing of industrial, commercial transportation and public utility enterprises. Plans for the project were announced recently by Peter Grimm, President of the Real Estate Board.

The statement of the board yesterday said, in part:

"The ultimate benefits, realty experts say, would not be confined to the facilitation of financing methods, but would extend to every phase of the business and would stimulate public interest in real estate as a whole by placing the flotation of its stock and bond issues on a stable and dependable basis. By providing a centralized and well regulated market for such stocks and bonds, it is argued, the new mart would make the securities more liquid and would thus encourage wider public participation in large building development and real estate enterprises.

"One phase of the exchange plan of outstanding significance is the protection that it affords the investor, for no issue of bonds or stocks will be offered on the floor until it has been thoroughly investigated and approved by the committees appointed for that purpose. In the case of bond issues in building projects, it is a condition of acceptance for listing that the preliminary appraisal must be made by the Real Estate Board's Appraisal Committee composed of recognized experts in the field of real estate valuation. On this score alone, it is intimated, the plan should receive the hearty endorsement and cooperation of the State's legal officials. Attorney General Albert Ottinger has long sought to devise methods for safeguarding the investing public against the promoters of flimsy and ill-conceived real estate ventures, and it is quite logical to assume that he will favor a scheme that should go far toward accomplishing the purposes of a blue sky law.

"The purchase of seats on the Exchange is limited to members of the Real Estate Board of New York in good standing. Membership is, for the present, limited to 250, but this may be extended by the Exchange's Board of Governors with the approval of the members. The price of the seats, or the initiation fee as it is termed, is $1,000.

"Real estate securities of all types issued in any part of the country may be listed on the Exchange, provided they conform to the high standards devised to test their soundness and pass the rigid scrutiny of the committee or committees entrusted with the duties of investigation. By no means one of the least important results from this broad field of activity will be the creation of a system of daily quotations establishing the current market price of sound securities, a thing which the real estate stock and bond market has long needed."

XIV

(Time allowed is 19 seconds)

Special to The New York Times.

WASHINGTON, Nov. 18.—American exports of finished manufactures during the fiscal year ending June 30 had a total value of $2,061,000,000, an increase of 4 per cent. over the previous year and 70 per cent. over the fiscal year 1922, Dr. Julius Klein, Director of the Bureau of Foreign and Domestic Commerce, declared in his annual report, made public today by the Commerce Department.

From one-seventh to one-eighth of the total farm production was marketed abroad, he said, representing the output of a million and a quarter persons while 8 or 9 per cent. of the output of factories is exported, representing the production of not far from a million industrial workers.

Workers in Export Production.

Dr. Klein gave the following summary of the workers employed in the more important lines of export trade, not including clerks and other salaried workers:

75,000 workers to produce machinery.
47,000 to turn out automobiles.
37,000 to prepare lumber and planing mill products.
31,000 to weave cotton goods.
26,000 to mine coal.
24,000 to manufacture iron and steel.
12,000 in petroleum refineries and many others in producing crude oil for export.
10,000 to compound chemical products.
8,000 in canning and preserving.
8,000 in rubber goods factories.
7,000 in copper smelters and many more in the mines.
6,000 in tanneries.
5,500 in knitting mills.
5,500 in tool and cutlery works.

Key to Domestic Prosperity.

"Should our foreign commerce suddenly be cut off," Dr. Klein added, "it would mean not merely displacement of a great army of workers, with its rebound on their families and dependents, but such a shock to industry, such a severe depression, as would throw out of employment also hundreds of thousands of those who are producing for purely domestic consumption."

Dr. Klein said that the Bureau of Foreign and Domestic Commerce had assisted directly in the forward march of export trade, and that American concerns were showing increased interest.

During the fiscal year ending June 30 sales and savings of $15,000,000 were reported by 800 exporters as traceable to the bureau's aids. On 3,000,000 occasions, or an average of 10,000 for each business day, the bureau rendered some kind of specific service.

XV
(Time allowed is 34 seconds)

Special to The New York Times.

WASHINGTON, Nov. 25.—The actual strength of the active army of the United States was 134,505 on June 30, 1928, exclusive of nurses, contract surgeons and West Point cadets, Major Gen. Lutz Wahl, the Adjutant General, stated in his annual report to the Secretary of War, made public today. There were 699 army nurses, 33 contract surgeons and 878 cadets, making a total of 136,115 in the military service.

By classes of personnel the army's strength was distributed as follows:

COMMISSIONED OFFICERS.

Regular Army (active list)	11,872
Philippine Scouts (active list)	94
Retired Regular Army, on active duty..	133
Retired Philippine Scouts, on active duty	13
Total Commissioned Officers	12,112

WARRANT OFFICERS.

Regular Army (active list)	1,208

ENLISTED MEN.

Regular Army (active list)	114,757
Philippine Scouts (active list)	6,400
Retired Regular Army, on active duty	28
Total enlisted men	121,185

Of the 134,505 officers and men 96,366 were serving in the continental United States, 14,083 in Hawaii, 8,605 in the Canal Zone, 310 in Alaska, 1,282 in Porto Rico, 11,343 in the Philippine Islands, including 6,486 officers and enlisted men of the Philippine Scouts; 979 in China, 7 in Europe attached to the Graves Registration Service, and 1,530 were either en route from one country to another, on leave of absence or serving as military attaches in foreign countries.

Sources of Officer Personnel.

Less than one-third of the 11,966 officers in the commissioned personnel of the regular army and Philippine Scouts were West Point graduates.

Almost as many officers came from civil life as from West Point. The sources of appointment were given as follows:

Civil life	3,428
Graduate, Military Academy	3,544
Enlisted man, Regular Army	1,119
Officer, National Army	253
Enlisted man, National Army	275
Officer, Reserve Corps	2,184
Enlisted man, Reserve Corps	205
Enlisted man, National Guard	271
Volunteer officer	43
Volunteer, enlisted man	16
Officer, National Guard	331
Warrant officer pay clerk, army field clerk, field clerk of Quartermaster Corps	48
Contract surgeon or veterinarian	144
Retired officer, restored to active list	16
Retired enlisted man	1
Public Health Service	1
Revenue Cutter Service	1
Coast and Geodetic Survey	2
Flying cadet	68
Officer, Philippine scouts	16
Total	11,966

The 3,428 officers appointed from civil life included, in addition to those who had no previous military service, men who have had service during the war with Spain, the World War or in the regular army, but who had returned to civil life.

During the fiscal year 162 commissioned officers were retired, 83 resigned, 14 were discharged, 2 were dropped as absent without leave, 5 were dismissed, 70 died and 33 retired officers previously assigned to active duty were relieved.

Results of Selective Recruiting.

"Intelligence tests introduced experimentally in several corps areas last year were put into general operation throughout the recruiting service beginning with the fiscal year ended June 30, 1928," said General Wahl, "and all new applicants for enlistment were subjected to these tests, which are designed primarily to aid in the elimination of undesirable applicants before their enlistment.

"As a result of the precautions taken, the percentage of desertions during the year again showed a decrease, having been 5.81 per cent, as compared with 6.07 per cent for the previous fiscal year.

"The losses from all causes among enlisted men during the year aggregated 58,914, by far the greater number having been discharged because of expiration of service."

The activities of the recruiting service were rewarded by the enlistment and re-enlistment of 56,748 men, including 1,148 for the Philippine Scouts. Of the 55,600 exclusive of the Philippine Scouts, General Wahl said, 52,097, or 93.7 per cent, were native-born Americans; 53,877 were white, including 476 Porto Ricans; 1,444 colored and 279 were of other races.

The aggregate strength of the Reserve Corps at the end of the fiscal year was 114,824, including 9,765 officers, who held commissions in both the National Guard and the Reserve Corps. This was a net increase of 4,810 during the fiscal year.

NOTE TO THE READER

Up to this point you have been increasing your skimming rate from 10 words per second in the first exercises to 20 in the last. You have found 20 words per second an almost impossible rate of skimming.

You ought now to be able to skim the following article moderately well at the rate of 10 words per second. Try to finish it in 12 minutes.

After you have skimmed this last long article, write or dictate the general content as you recall it.

XVI[1]

The skeptical and well informed reader who has been following these investigations must long ago have raised his voice in protest against one glaring oversight in my survey.

"You have ignored the farmer! You consider all the professions, business, manufacturing and scientific research," he

[1] PITKIN, WALTER B., "The Twilight of the American Mind," Chap. XVIII, Simon and Schuster, 1928.

is saying. "But you never seek openings for superior minds in agriculture. Isn't this rather absurd? Farming, if done correctly, calls for a higher order of all-around ability. For centuries untold it occupied the best minds. Why not today?"

I admit that I have left the farmer out of the reckoning thus far. But I have done so for a peculiar reason, which must now be declared. My approach to the problem of the superior man and his future is sternly realistic. I try to observe and deal with things as they are, first of all; then with things as they seem likely to become soon; and finally with things as we may be able to shape them to suit our own sweet wills. I am not even remotely interested in ideals, as the genuine idealists think of them. So swiftly moves the world of men and affairs that it is folly to strive to look ahead more than a few decades—and greater folly still to plan ahead for more than a few years. Twenty months from this moment, some Bessarabian agronomist may hit upon the long sought method of breeding soil bacteria in quantity; and before 1930, the world's food supply will have become inexhaustible and cheaper than the very dirt from which it springs. But why dally over dreams of such miracles? Why not study and plan today strictly in the light of realities as they now are? Why not compute probabilities on the firm basis of certainties?

In this spirit I look at farming and the farmer. And I see no hope for our Best Minds in agriculture. That is to say, I see no hope for hundreds of thousands of superior people seeking better *careers* on farms than they now find in cities. Relative to our total population there are too many superior people already engaged in agriculture, trying to make money at it. Thousands of them must leave their acres, in order to find the satisfaction they seek in life. Why? The answer is rather complicated. It cannot be otherwise. For the world situation in agriculture is a maze through which few economists and still fewer social scientists can thread their way. To grasp it thoroughly, one must have lived on farms and visited many other farms in widely differing parts of the world.

Behind all the flurries in crop prices, behind all droughts, floods, forest fires, insect plagues, partisan politics, stock swindles, and other disasters that strike the farmers now and then, there is to be found a fundamental state of affairs which has driven and will continue to drive from the farms all persons of superior intelligence except the tiny minority who enjoy farm life and do not look to it for their chief income.   This state of affairs is one which, prior to the twentieth century, drove the world's farmers steadily downward into the coolie class.   And now, with the advent of super-machinery and super-organization, it will drive 95 per cent of all farmers still faster into cooliedom, while it will slowly lift the remaining 5 per cent into the exalted position of farm corporation stockholders, owners, and managers.

First lay firm hold of a few elemental facts about the farmer, facts which all economists and other observers agree upon. Most important of all is the fact that the American farmer is neither a capitalist nor a laborer in the true economic sense. That is to say, his business—if we can call it such without laughing—is not run as any modern business man runs his own; nor is his labor rewarded on the same basis and principle as the industrial worker's is.   The farmer is neither fish, flesh, nor fowl.

As business men figure, the farmer makes no profit whatsoever. Rather does he incur every year an appalling loss.   A sound business must pay a normal rate of interest on all its capital and must pay wages to all who work for it.   Only after these and other expenses have been met, is there anything left for true profit.   Now, so far as anybody knows, there isn't a farmer in North America who can run his acres on this basis and come out even at the year's end; and if there are a few, the odds are a hundred to one that they could not show a true profit on a ten-year average.

The recent analysis made by the National Industrial Conference Board reveals that, since 1920, the American farmer has been averaging only 4 per cent return on his capital investment. His return on operation is only 2 per cent.   That is, if he rents a farm and spends money on crops, he gets only this microscopic reward.   What the Conference Board does not mention is that *the farm operator makes this 2 per cent only by taking out not a cent for salary for himself, as operator.*   What a dolt he is to accept this basis of remuneration! What a fool to stick at such unprofitable toil!

If the American farmer paid himself for his own services no more than the unskilled laborer in the city receives, he would not have a cent left to pay interest on his capital investment or to employ other help or to do anything else. As a business man he is a total failure from the outset. And as a laborer he is lower than the meanest ditch digger and garbage collector on a city wage. Measured by modern economics, he is a standing joke. The only wonder is that he continues to stand.

His business, if we may call it that ironically, is more hazardous than most others. Yet he never takes out of it any high profit that rewards him for his great risks. And, as I shall later show in some detail, the only gain he has ever made is the little represented by the increased value of his land.

In 1923, the total wages of the 8,778,950 workers in all American factories amounted to $11,009,298,000.

This sum almost precisely equals that which American farmers lose every year by growing and selling crops, if we reckon costs and profits as manufacturers and other business men do.

Every year American corporations distribute dividends amounting to something between two and three billion dollars.

Every year farm land crops are damaged to this same extent— two to three billion dollars—by soil erosion, removal of soil fertility, and insect pests.

If farmers were in a position to sell their products on the same basis with manufacturers in other lines, and if they were likewise able to make selling prices take proper care of depreciation of their productive property, basic living costs would rise enormously in all cities; and the industrial system as now developed in Europe and America would be impossible. Instead of our country consisting, as it now does, of three major classes, rural coolies, urban workers at or just above the subsistence level, and a very prosperous upper economic class of about 2,000,000 people, we should have virtually only one class of moderately prosperous citizens in town and country, the very rich class then being so small in numbers as to be economically negligible.

The more intelligent men and women all over the world
are deserting farms.   This appears in the dwindling production of
basic crops.   The farmers of the world are producing today less
than they did before the World War.

Here are the most significant figures:

Crop	1913	1927[1]
Wheat	4,087,000,000 bu.	3,390,784,000 bu.
Corn	3,743,000,000 bu.	3,266,150,000 bu.
Oats	4,798,500,000 bu.	3,440,075,000 bu.
Rye	1,893,000,000 bu.	883,191,000 bu.
Barley	1,779,000,000 bu.	1,188,165,000 bu.
Cotton	26,259,000 bales	15,100,100 bales
Swine	2,881,000,000 head	2,837,000,000 head (1924)

[1] 1927 estimates published by the International Institute of Agriculture,
Rome.

Only three major crops have not dwindled thus.   They
are potatoes, wool, and tobacco.   The last is sinister, when we
consider that it is one of the worst wasters of soil fertility in the
world.

To grasp the full meaning of these figures, you must understand
that, in spite of the huge losses caused by the World War and the
influenza epidemic, the population of the world in 1927 greatly
exceeded that of 1913.   Also keep before you the fact that
European agriculture had, in 1927, recovered from the after-
effects of the war and was on a new normal level.

The entire world now stands on the threshold of an Agrarian
Revolution which careful analysis reveals to be the last and
greatest phase of the Industrial Revolution which came to its
first focus in the late eighteenth century.   Little by little the
methods of our money and profit economy are undermining the
old and hopelessly barbaric type of agriculture which has prevailed all over the world since man first hit upon the most deeply
revolutionary scheme in his entire career, tilling the soil.   For
centuries uncounted, farming has been a way of life, not a business in the modern sense.   Men lived in the country, raised their
own food, grew their own wool for clothing dug holes in the
ground to get cool, clean water, and chopped down ancient trees

for firewood and house timbers. Their wives milked cows and goats, churned, washed dishes, raised ten or twelve children, and drudged along dully till they dropped dead over the kitchen sinks. It was just Life.

Did these primitive rustics ever figure as the smallest town retailer or shop owner must? Did they reckon up their invested capital and then set down interest charges for it as an item to be met out of sales? Did they carefully compute depreciation of soils through erosion and the removal of fertility in crops? Did they ever pay themselves, their wives and their grown children wages as city business men do when they employ their families? The very questions answer themselves. We have about 6,500,-000 farms in the country today; of these, not 5,000 are or could be run as a city store, factory, mill, or other enterprise must be, to keep out of bankruptcy.

From the point of view of anybody who thinks in terms of modern economics, all farming by individual owners and operators on a few hundred acres or less is simply preposterous. Too many managers relative to the number of workers! Think of it! We have only 200,000 manufacturing establishments, of which thousands are under central office management; but we have 6,500,000 separately operated farms. Now if there is anything sure in vocational tests, it is the very small percentage of competent managers that can be found throughout our adult population. If we may judge by several broad samplings recently made, not more than three skilled laborers out of every hundred have any ambition to become foremen or superintendents; they prefer their routine work under orders, they dislike giving orders and running other people. And their dislike is generally based on a sound instinct which quietly tells them that they are not competent managers. It is very safe to assume that not more than one man in every hundred is sufficiently gifted as an executive to run any enterprise easily and well. This suggests that not more than 65,000 American farmers are able to run their estates so as to make money. And most of these are not making anything like the money they ought to, because they are in active competition against 6,435,000 small farmers who run their business so poorly that they gladly sell crops at a loss and are content to go on working without getting even so much as the wages of a city ditch digger.

A business man cannot compete against a coolie. This is the root of the Agrarian Revolution in our own country. It is the primary cause of all the agitation behind the Farm Bloc. And it must continue to be that until we have settled, once and for all time, the burning issue: shall we turn American agriculture into a sound business or into ancient peasantry? There is no third course. And there can be no lasting compromise. Just as our nation, in the day before the Civil War, could not exist half slave and half free, so now we cannot exist half business and half peasant. If we do not face this squarely, we shall soon be facing a social revolution which, in its way, may prove almost as disastrous as the Civil War.

Now how does this bear on our immediate problem? Well, during the next twenty or thirty years, the Agrarian Revolution will grow steadily worse, if not from the social then at least from the business point of view. There will be no fresh opportunities for anybody, dull or clever, in American agriculture— unless it be the process server and the sheriff. After that, what? Things will settle down in either one of the two ways I have named. We may put all agriculture on the basis of Old World peasantry, or we may put it all on a business basis.

If we revert to peasantry, the outcome will be essentially as in England today. There about nine out of every ten acres of farm land are owned by a few immensely rich landlords and rented out to small peasants who toil fourteen or fifteen hours a day, live as no city dweller would consent to live, and slowly sink to lower and lower intelligence levels, as several recent English surveys have shown. School children in the rural sections of Yorkshire and Northumberland score much more poorly than do city and suburban children. (The one exception is the very remote rural school, from which better types have not been drawn off to city work.) What chance is there in such a system of agriculture for our Best Minds? None whatsoever!

Suppose, on the other hand, that our industrialists, bankers, social workers, and politicians join hands in lifting American agriculture out of its present degradation into a sound economic position.

It is more than possible that, as the Agrarian Revolution proceeds, intelligent men will come to the belief that food must be treated as a public utility just as water, gas, electricity, and transportation now are. Then the regulation of food production and food distribution will begin on a scale undreamed of today even by the wildest radicals in the Farm Bloc. Probably it will begin with some kind of regional franchises, such as a contract between a city and some large corporation for the annual food supply on a price basis which guarantees to the corporation a fair net profit, and to the citizens a sliding scale of standardized food prices fitted nicely to production and distribution costs.

At one stroke, such a move would do away with a horde of nuisances. The present preposterous methods of food marketing would vanish over night. Food would be delivered as gas now is, by the corporation itself under strict contract with penalty clauses which would protect each householder. Each consumer would pay strictly for what he used and for no more; and the quality and quantity of his purchases would be absolutely guaranteed. I venture to assert that the city which is first to introduce such a system will instantly gain a lead over rival communities in the way of attracting superior working-men and factories. This will force other cities to follow suit. And the upshot of it all will be the rapid multiplication of food service corporations analogous to the United Fruit Company on the production side and to Childs' Restaurants on the distribution side. Then the small farmer will disappear like snow under sudden sun.

It seems more than reasonable that the trend toward large corporation farming may come, not directly but rather by way of experiments in regional coöperation. Individual small farmers, urged on by bitter necessity, may band together for self-help; and, having so banded, they will slowly learn that central management is vastly more efficient than simple coöperation. They will also learn, though perhaps by trial and error, that some of their number manage affairs far better than others, and that such superior managers can earn more for all concerned than the coöperators can earn individually. From this stage of enlightenment it will be an easy journey into the fair land of corporation farming. Instead of five hundred barns scattered all over a county, there will be five immense structures equipped with all the conveniences and fire-protection equipment. Instead of there being five hundred houses there will be perhaps twenty fine ones on the acreage, strategically located, while the stockholders who do not work on the property live in near-by towns— or even in New York or Paris, for that matter. Instead of five overworked and underpaid country doctors, plodding the back roads in the dark and the storm, to seek out the distant sick, there will be a county medical center where the best of equipment and specialists will be ever on hand for immediate service, twenty-four hours a day. So too with veterinary service and all other basic necessities of rural life.

Coöperation is growing more and more popular. It is infinitely better than the pioneer type of stubborn individualism that has prevailed in America. It represents, however, the highest level which the peasantry of Europe has been able to reach, after centuries of struggle. It has gone about as far as it can go in Siberia and Denmark, where the dairy farmers especially have greatly bettered themselves through their unions. But such organizations are inferior to the Western corporations in every respect. They are slower in action, less competent to plan far ahead, less daring in their programs of improvement and experimentation, and less adequately financed for large operations. Above all, they cannot take full advantage of modern inventions and methods, chiefly because, at the bottom of every coöperative, you find a collection of individual operators who refuse to be graded and assigned to work that barely employs their mental and physical abilities.

In a few spots of our own Middle West we see how necessity has started farm owners in the right direction, in spite of themselves. As farmers have been failing right and left out there, their acres have been thrown back on the banks to whom they owed money or on mortgage holders who were themselves retired farmers. Merely to salvage their investments the assignees have, in a conspicuous instance or two, called in a well trained farm manager and turned over to him dozens or even scores of farms in one region with orders to make the most of them. Such huge profits have been earned, after one or two seasons of struggle to get the deteriorated land into shape, that other owners of farms have imitated the procedure. In Iowa, for instance, men who have long been leasing to tenant farmers find it more profitable to alter the leases so as to leave the entire management in the hands of themselves or some agronomist, while the tenant simply carries out instructions and takes his share of the profit. This happens to be astonishingly like the newest form of employee profit-sharing adopted by progressive corporations; and there are reasons to believe that it may turn out to the advantage of all concerned, while serving as a natural transition to corporation farming.

Whatever may prove to be the wisest methods of accomplishing it, we may be sure that an essential feature of the final reform program will be an enormous reduction in the number of farms and farm managers. Instead of 6,500,000 farms, we shall have perhaps 200,000. By averaging only 2,500 acres of tilled land each, these large and well managed establishments will take care of our entire improved acreage, which is around 500,000,000 acres. Adequately capitalized and scientifically managed, the 200,000 farms of the New Order will derive fully 25 per cent more food products from their acreage than our coolies now get. They will employ about the same number of farm hands per production unit as farmers now do; about one man for every 26 acres of tilled land. And nearly all of the small farmers who are now starving and overworking themselves and their families will become decent laborers, well fed, well housed, and generally well cared for.

Many forces are now at work toward this wholesome end. Look at the recent colossal investment of the Brotherhood of Locomotive Engineers. After having sold the controlling interest in the $40,000,000 Equitable Building in New York City, it decided to invest no less than $10,000,000 in an immense farm colony in Florida. A tract of 30,000 acres was bought south of Tampa, houses and hotels and highways were built, and the balance of the land divided into five- and ten-acre farms for intensive winter truck gardening under central management but with individual ownership of the farms. The site was selected after a study revealed that the average annual profit in the region over a five-year period, good years and bad, good farmers and bad all lumped into the measure, was $479.73.

Money will slowly flow into regions of high yield like this one. It will never flow into regions of poor yield and no profit. This means that millions of acres now under coolie cultivation will in time revert to grass or timber or even swamp, while the best millions of acres will become modern food factories, well capitalized and well managed, with all the new methods of unit operation and mass production and mass distribution adapted as far as possible to the industry.

And how about jobs for our Best Minds? I cannot see where even one can be adequately employed. Good managers, yes. Superintendents, yes. Salesmen, yes. Accountants, yes. Gang foremen, yes. And there the list of superior workers ends, save for a sprinkling of research scientists who might number as high as 2,500 or 3,000 for the entire country. These would be agronomists of the highest type, some of them specializing more narrowly in economic entomology, soil chemistry, or climatology, and so on. They would easily handle all the problems that might arise. For, as you must keep in mind whenever we talk about the productivity of the Best Minds, what one man discovers by scientific research almost immediately becomes common property. If we have five hundred entomologists all working on the boll weevil and the Japanese beetle, but under various agencies public and private, they are practially all working for everybody who needs their services. Their discoveries are promptly published, and their opinions on special application techniques may be had for the asking.

I conclude then that a careful job analysis of farming as it may become in the near future reveals no appreciable number of openings for men and women of 130 I.Q. or better. The best we can say is that many of our Best Minds who enjoy the country life and have other means of support besides tilling the soil may prefer to live on small farms, or even to own one of the great corporation farms of the future, in part or in whole. I dare say the countryside of 1975 will be dotted with the homes of such persons. But they do not count in our present reckoning. For we are seeking jobs which demand the highest intelligence and which will give the jobholder a living suited to his nature and nurture.

So much for the state of affairs in the days of our grandchildren. Now let us glance at conditions closer at hand. Let us see whether our Best Minds may not find at least a temporary refuge and profit in farming before the Agrarian Revolution comes to an end in days far off. This investigation must be made largely because there is a strong belief among some vocational psychologists and more progressive farmers that the general level of intelligence is steadily rising among our agrarians; that living conditions are improving; and that there is a genuine opportunity for the higher mental types of Americans to go into farming. Sundry well informed farm journal editors, as well as Farm Bloc leaders, have been assuring their followers for some years that this upward trend is going on and must continue. It sounds as if thousands of Best Minds might find themselves in modern farming.

In this they have been supported by sundry radical eugenists and by some vocational psychologists. Let us consider the arguments of these latter.

Huntington and Whitney reason as follows:

In order that agriculture may occupy its rightful position in this country, what proportion of the farmers ought to be of the Builder type? Take, for example, a township where the township consists mainly of one or two hundred families of farmers. If such a township is to prosper and maintain the best American standards, it obviously needs at least a few local leaders, and a much larger number of lieutenants who follow the leaders promptly. Leaders and followers alike must keep up more or less with the affairs of their state and country, and even of the world, as well as with local affairs. Otherwise they cannot judge how a given policy will affect not only themselves and their neighbors but the whole community . . .

In addition to this, they . . . must keep up with the march of events in their own occupation. They must be able to weigh the different accounts of a new invention . . . a new breed of cattle, a new crop, or a new way of caring for the forest. Builders with a talent for organization are also needed . . .

If our farmers are to maintain what we proudly call the American standards, if they are to make a permanent success of local self-government, and render farming a highly respected and desirable profession, at least one farmer in ten and probably one in five ought to be a Builder. That means that one or two million farmers ought to be Builders—let us say a million and a half.[1]

The trouble with this vision is that it lacks a sound basis in economic fact, first of all.   A standard township of 36 square miles contains 23,040 acres, of which fully one-third must be devoted to woodlots, highways, water courses or ponds, grazing fields, and sites for houses, barns, sheds and the like. This leaves about 15,000 acres to be tilled, provided the soil is fit for tillage.   We may assume, as a general average, that not more than two-thirds of the 15,000 acres will earn a fair profit when tilled.   I suspect I am making too liberal an allowance here; but let it stand, for the argument's sake.   Now, a poor small farmer would till all the acres, regardless of profit; but a farm corporation would not.   It would till only the 10,000 profitable acres.   And a tract of this size is almost ideal for large-scale farming of the sort which will come more and more into vogue. What, now, will be the typical population of such a township when the Agrarian Revolution shall have been completed successfully?

A general manager, three or four farm superintendents under him, one agronomist perhaps, a chief mechanic in charge of the big machines, and beyond that nobody save common laborers. For a farm is a factory, and it must follow the inexorable law of the factory; division of labor, unit operations, and the allocation of tasks to those who are not superior to them but barely competent.   By no other way can the American farmer rise to enjoy the high standard of living which his brother in the city has long enjoyed.

Instead of there being one superior leader among farmers for every five or ten of our present farming population, there ought not be more than one such leader for every fifty or a hun. dred.   Not a million and a half for the country at large, then, as Huntington and Whitney estimate, but rather around 150,000

[1] "The Builders of America," pp. 7 and 8.

at the very highest. And, of this number, not more than one-fifth need to be even Second-Best Minds. Leaders, yes. Intellects, no.

Now let us look at the psychologist's argument in favor of future improvements in farmers' intelligence.

Donald Laird, the vocational psychologist, has remarked that the tendency among farmers must be toward an ever higher intelligence level, as a result of natural selection.

The mental demands placed upon the farmer have rapidly increased. The mental demands upon the industrial worker have been growing less and less. So it is into industrial work that the farmer who cannot keep up with the race enters. There his thinking is done for him, and his work is much less complicated and taxing on the mind. It is a process of social natural selection with the intelligence of the remaining farmers increasing each week, due to their ranks being deserted by those less able to meet the increasing mental demands.

So far so good! Laird correctly depicts the trend. But he shows us only one phase of it. It is also true that, for every four or five inferior farmers who go to town to work in mill or factory, one superior farmer also goes because he understands how cruelly handicapped the individual farmer is in the struggle for an American living standard. And this superior emigrant usually has the highest energy and ambition. He is one of the country's *élite*. Old farmers call him "restless," "a wild colt," and "a fellow with no dirt sense nor horse sense." And they are right.

His mind works far too fast for farm work. The ideal farmer is, as all competent observers agree, a man of much slower mental velocities than the typical city business man. To deal with horses, cows, and poultry, you need a more gently moving mind and hand than you do when running a sewing machine or a lathe. So too in handling crops, in planning rotations, and in going through the ordinary day's work on the farm. Centuries of natural selections have thus weeded from the farms the nervous, the impatient, and the high-speed types of humanity. Slow caution and gentleness and easy-going ambition characterize the successful farmers.

This, by the way, accounts largely for the extraordinarily poor showing of the farmers in the Army intelligence tests. Out of forty-two occupations they ranked fifth from the bottom. To be sure, this was partly caused by the fact that a considerable percentage of moron and near-moron farm hands were classified as farmers. This was as absurd as it would have been to classify all men who work in automobile factories as manufacturers, or all school janitors as educators. But the city men who ran the tests did not understand this; hence the absurdity of their findings. On the other hand, it cannot be doubted that the genuine farmers did score badly according to the tests. But they did so chiefly because the Army tests, in their original form (now abandoned in large measure), were really *mental speed* tests. As Cattell and other psychologists have since pointed out, they measured alertness rather than fundamental intelligence. We know that high intelligence may move slowly as well as rapidly. We know that, for some kinds of work and responsibilities, the slow sort is infinitely better than the swift. Above all, does the slow mind prosper in farming.

We see then a steady and presumably swelling exodus of two male types from the farms; the inferior and the overalert minds. How about the female emigrants? Here we lack detailed information that is nation-wide and statistical. But the run of personal testimony everywhere is most uniform, as well as alarming. Here are samples:

The clever girls and the pretty girls in our country all leave the farm as soon as they can. They will not stand the drudgery of housework on a farm. They see their mothers overworked, getting nowhere except into early graves, and having precious little time for even the simplest of life's enjoyments. Why should a girl stay on the farm anyhow?

The young men who stay on the farms and get along well are marrying mostly Scandinavian peasant girls. The better class of American girls won't marry a herd of cattle and five hundred hens and a quarter-section.

The small farmers around us seem to have married mostly stupid women, dull drudges who are content to live in the kitchen and cook and scrub all day.

A Pennsylvania school teacher caps the climax:

I have visited most of the farms in the township within range of my school. Fully half of the housewives I have met are distinctly subnormal in their intelligence. Many of them are complete morons, while half a dozen are true feebleminded types. The shocking thing, though, is that many of these inferior creatures are the wives of the solid, hard-working and competent small farmers. What will their children be? Just peasants, men with hoes and women with mops!

My personal impression, gathered from hundreds of farms, is pretty much the same. The focus of agrarian decay, on the human side, is not in the men. It is in the women. And all the current forces of American life are combining to draw, ever faster and faster, the refined, intelligent, particular woman from the countryside. Life, even on a good farm, bears heavily or the woman. Look on the picture of the drudgery!

The Department of Agriculture, a few years ago, surveyed 10,015 farm homes in 33 states, not including the South, where rural conditions are much worse than elsewhere. The aim was to see just how the farmer's wife spends her day, what facilities she enjoys and lacks, and what the causes of her discontent are. As you scan the findings, bear in mind that the homes described are not those of the poverty-stricken hill billies and white trash. They are typical farm homes in the prosperous farming sections of our land.

The working day of the average farm woman proved to be 11.3 hours, the year around. In summer it is 13.12 hours! Out of every 100 women, 87 never took any vacation. On a summer day, the farmer's wife can find only 1.6 hours of leisure; in winter she manages to get 2.4 hours a day for herself.

Six out of every ten do not even have a pump in their kitchens but must walk some distance to the spring or well to fetch water for cooking their meals and for washing. Each woman has, on the average, a seven-room house to care for; kerosene lamps to trim and fill; family washing to do, without any washing machines; and, just to keep her out of mischief, all the family sewing and darning to do.

In addition to caring for the house, cooking all meals and caring for the children, the farmer's wife usually takes full charge of the poultry and does all the baking for family and farm hands.   One woman out of four also helps care for the live-stock.   One out of every five also toils for six weeks each year in the fields, helping with the planting and harvesting.   One out of every three helps with the milking.   And more than half of them all must do all the churning.

How can intelligent or frail women endure this?   They must leave!

One further important fact must be added to complete the picture of natural selection.   There is an intelligence level below which cityward migration does not occur.   Laird seems to think that all sorts of inferior farmers and farm workers tend to leave the country.   But this is assuredly not true.   All over the United States we find hordes far too inert, too dumb, and too ignorant to wander from their habitat in search of something better. Their accepted living standard, low as it is, suffices.   Not only is their intelligence far below normal, but their temperament is such that scarcely any hardships of daily life can stir them to to discontent, still less to emigration.   They are apathetic morons.   Thousands of them dwell in the older farm regions of the North Atlantic states; and their number in the Midwest and South is steadily growing.   I have met and talked with hundreds of them in New England, New Jersey, Pennsylvania, and the back valleys of the Appalachians.   Whole families of them now living within fifty miles of Wall Street have never had ambition to visit any large city.   Education cannot improve them. Put clean clothes on their backs, and they will be filthy within a week.   Teach them all the virtues, and they will go serenely along their old paths.   They remember little and suffer less. In a word, they are ideal low-grade farm hands, fit for the drudgery of the onion field and the barn yard.   The few who have been tempted or forced to try work in the towns come back in a hurry; for the speed and the noise and the pressure of town work are too much for their simple nervous systems.

Now let us assemble the parts of this natural selection pattern. Two asymmetrical distributions develop, one for each sex. Among the men, those who tend to leave the farm are (1) the superintelligent who find in farm work nothing to occupy their minds, (2) the high-strung and very alert of considerable intelligence, (3) the energetic subintelligent, and (4) the physically frail of all intelligence levels except the very lowest. Among women, the emigrants are chiefly (1) the superintelligent, (2) the superior intelligent, whether (*a*) alert or (*b*) apathetic-slow, (3) the average intelligent, especially those who are sensitive or rather frail. In other words, all the very low-grade types of both men and women tend to stay in the country; all the very alert, sensitive, and physically delicate men and women tend to leave; and more kinds of intelligent men remain on the farms than kinds of intelligent women. In the long run, then, the currents of farm life seem to be carrying us toward a peculiarly complicated state of affairs. The mental level of farm operators is now rising, as Laird has said. At the same time the level of women in the families of these operators is declining, though just how much or how fast we cannot estimate. As the living standards of ordinary workers in American cities rise, however, we may be sure that the shift of superior farm girls and women to the cities will grow apace. On the other hand, the lowest grade of farm hands not only holds its own as to numbers but is increasing, especially in the poorer farming regions. And the more an agricultural region deteriorates, the larger will this degraded class become.

Now, it would be interesting but futile to speculate on the outcome of this differentiation into two intelligence classes over a period of centuries. Let us be content to sense its drift for the next few decades. Surely it is carrying us in the direction of the next great advance which will mark the arrival of the Agrarian Revolution. It sweeps onward—and, I feel sure, also upward—toward corporation farming on a scale hitherto undreamed of. It is bringing to its end the prescientific epoch of personal farming, small-capital farming, and peonage.

As the intelligence of the farm operators rises during the next thirty, forty, or fifty years, and as their relative number declines, is not the stage plainly set for more and more intelligent coöperation? And must not the outcome of intelligent coöperation be, whether in its legal form or not, the adaptation of all the methods of industrial organization and machinery and techniques to farm problems? Must not the "unit operation" be adopted, as far as it can be, on the farm? Must not labor selection there be made on the same principle as in the factory? "Never allow a worker to do a piece of work which a less able man can do as well!" In farm work this has one inevitable meaning and application. It must lead in the long run to the complete separation of farm management from farm work. It must lead to a working ratio of field laborer to manager-expert more or less like that which is found the best in our factories; say, from twenty to fifty unskilled or semi-skilled toilers for each high-grade superintendent or expert. But this can be accomplished only with expensive machines and expensive organizers. In it the small farmer of today has no place. Hence he must go the way of the dinosaur and the dodo. Or, if he stays at farming, he must do so because he enjoys it as a way of life, not as a source of income.

And now we are back to the prediction I made a few minutes ago about the Agrarian Revolution! Whether we look to the inner evolution of farming, as now carried on, or to the immense external pressures and attractions which constantly alter the make-up of rural population and the pattern of rural work, we see the same final consequences. No chance for many Best Minds!

THE RACING EYE

Just to show you how useless it is to read faster than you take in the content, let me give you a simple test.

Here follows a page of fairly clear facts. See how fast you can read it. Probably you will dash through it in less than 50 seconds; and you may cover it in a few as 35 seconds.

The instant you have finished reading it, turn the page. Then try to write a summary of what you have read.

Have Your Paper And Pencil Ready Before You Begin!

A ski is a wooden snow-shoe. Implements for this purpose were used in ancient times. Xenephon describes the skin shoes with which the horses of the Armenians were shod. Snow-shoes have long been used by the Mongols of northwestern Asia. They were common in Scandinavia long before the Christian era.

Ancient skis were elongated, curved frames covered with leather. Those of the Skrid-Finnen of the sixteenth century were leather shoes, pointed at the toe, into which the feet were thrust up to the ankles. Modern skis are long, narrow, pieces of ash, oak, spruce or hickory, pointed and turned up for about a foot at the toe. Their length is usually the distance their wearer can reach upwards with his hand. Their width at the broadest part is about five inches, and their greatest thickness (just under the foot) about an inch and a quarter, tapering toward both ends. The under surface is usually smooth, although some skis have slight grooves to prevent the snow caking. They are kept in condition by oiling and waxing. Paraffin wax is used to produce a very highly polished surface, which greatly increases the speed of the runner. Long strips of sealskin are sometimes attached to the under side, to prevent side-slipping and assist the climber to make a direct ascent.

The skis are fitted to the feet by straps. There are a very large number of bindings, the commonest among novice runners being the huitfeld, and the most popular with experienced skiers the B. B. This is a metal binding without any straps, relying entirely on a hook-and-eye arrangement at the toe of the boot. The boots are made of deer hide. For use with the heel-strap bindings have specially shaped heels with a groove which hold the strap in place.

On level ground the skis glide evenly over the snow without being lifted from it, the heels being raised with each forward movement. Long gliding steps can be taken without fatigue, the runner having a stick about four feet or five feet long in each hand, to assist progression. These sticks have a spiked end, about seven inches above which a metal disk is fixed to prevent the stick sinking into the snow. Going down hill the skier places one foot slightly ahead of the other and runs in a crouched position with the feet close together and body leaning forward. A single staff was formerly used as a brake in coasting downhill, but the popularity of two sticks used chiefly for assistance in uphill work, but also for balance on the descent, is now the rule.

Now for the second exercise. Here follows another page with almost exactly the same number of facts. Read it as slowly as you can, without actually re-reading each line. You ought to be able to slow down to about 160 seconds.

Snow is crystallized vapour in the air. It forms at various heights according to latitude and temperature. It forms in great quantities within high clouds in all latitudes. Although most common to the polar region, it forms even in greater quantity within the north temperate regions.

Over the polar regions and upon lofty mountains, perpetual snow covers most of the land. On mountain or plateau regions therein, and on high mountains elsewhere, it accumulates to such depth that the pressure of the upper masses forms glaciers, sometimes covering thousands of square miles. It often accumulates to a depth of from one to four or more feet during the winter. The amount of snowfall varies markedly upon mountain tops and other locations even in the same parallel degree of latitude.

The crystalline varieties of snow are generally transparent and have brilliant facets that reflect light. They vary in size from one-one-hundredth to one-half inch in diameter, and fall to earth either singly or in flakes. Flake formation occurs usually during the mild, moist snowfalls at a ground temperature of 32 degrees or above. Cold clouds, always relatively dry, tend to produce smaller, slow-growing and solid types of crystal. Warmer clouds contain more moisture, tending to produce the larger, fast-growing, branchy type of crystals. The nuclear atoms of water are so arranged as to tend to cause the formation of triangular or hexagonal forms of snow crystals.

Most crystals of snow can be roughly grouped into two main classes, columnar and tabular. The columnar forms are hexagonal columns. The tabular shapes, whether solid or branching, form on a thin, tabular plane. There are many irregular snow forms—icy spicules, frost-like forms, etc. During extreme cold or snowfall from high, cold clouds, tiny columns and solid hexagonal or triangular plates are common.

Most snowfall shows branching tabular forms, granular forms, plates with branching exteriors, plate forms columns, needle forms, compound forms. The columnar and needle-like forms are much alike, varying in size, length, thickness, etc. Compound crystals show much greater variation in size, aspect, interior details, etc., of the end plates.

By far the most important and beautiful snow crystals are those of the tabular class. These crystals have delicate, starry, branching forms, solid plate forms and others equally beautiful. They are far more beautiful than crystals of any mineral species.

Snow crystals crystallize while floating about unsupported in the air. The atoms and molecules of snow move more freely while arranging themselves in crystal form than is possible when most crystals are formed. Snow crystals are formed directly from the atoms and molecules of water floating between the cloud droplets, as is illustrated by the fact that scanty snowfalls frequently occur from clear skies.

As a result of unfavorable cloud conditions, such as winds, overcrowding, the presence of fluid cloud droplets, etc., most tabular snow crystals fail to attain their natural beauty and symmetry. There is doubtless a somewhat invariable law of distribution of the various types of snow.

Tabular snow crystals are beautiful in outline and in interior design. This is due to the presence of air tubes and shadings in them, which appear dark when seen under certain conditions. These interior air tubes and shadings frequently appear as tiny rods, dots, lines, etc., in a symmetrical manner.

PART V

EXERCISES FOR PRACTICE

Here are some exercises for practice reading. They represent four degrees of difficulty. Before each group the reading rate which you should be able to attain is indicated. Perhaps you cannot read it at this speed at first. But you ought to *after* you have worked for two months on this book.

Make other exercises for yourself, classifying the reading matter as it is done here. Time yourself accurately. Keep this up for four to eight weeks.

LIGHT READING

(Reading rate about five or six words per second)

Exercise 1

(You should be able to read this poem in about 2 minutes)

ODE TO THE WEST WIND

O wild West Wind, thou breath of Autumn's being,
Thou, from whose unseen presence the leaves dead
Are driven, like ghosts from an enchanter fleeting,

Yellow, and black, and pale, and hectic red,
Pestilence-stricken multitudes: O thou
Who chariotest to their dark wintry bed

The wing'd seeds, where they lie cold and low
Each like a corpse within its grave, until
Thine azure sister of the Spring shall blow

Her clarion o'er the dreaming earth, and fill
(Driving sweet buds like flocks to feed in air)
With living hues and odors plain and hill:

Wild Spirit, which art moving everywhere;
Destroyer and preserver; hear, oh, hear!

Thou on whose stream, mid the steep sky's commotion
Loose clouds like earth's decaying leaves are shed,
Shook from the tangled boughs of Heaven and Ocean,

Angels of rain and lightning: there are spread
On the blue surface of thine airy surge,
Like the bright hair uplifted from the head

Of some fierce Mænad, even from the dim verge
Of the horizon to the zenith's height,
The locks of the approaching storm.   Thou dirge

Of the dying year, to which this closing night
Will be the dome of a vast sepulchre,
Vaulted with all thy congregated might

Of vapors, from whose solid atmosphere
Black rain, and fire, and hail will burst: oh, hear!

Thou who didst waken from his summer dreams
The blue Mediterranean, where he lay,
Lulled by the coil of his crystalline streams,

Beside a pumice isle in Baiæ's bay,
And saw in sleep old palaces and towers
Quivering within the wave's intenser day,

All overgrown with azure moss and flowers
So sweet the sense faints picturing them! thou
For whose path the Atlantic's level powers

Cleave themselves into chasms, while far below
The sea-blooms and the oozy woods which wear
The sapless foliage of the ocean know

Thy voice, and suddenly grow gray with fear,
And tremble and despoil themselves: oh, hear!

If I were a dead leaf thou mightest bear;
If I were a swift cloud to fly with thee;
A wave to pant beneath thy power, and share

The impulse of thy strength, only less free
Than thou, O uncontrollable!   If even
I were as in my boyhood, and could be

The comrade of thy wanderings over heaven,
As then, when to outstrip thy skyey speed
Scarce seemed a vision; I would ne'er have striven

As thus with thee in prayer in my sore need.
Oh, lift me as a wave, a leaf, a cloud!
I fall upon the thorns of life!   I bleed!

A heavy weight of hours has chained and bowed
One too like thee: tameless, and swift, and proud.

Make me thy lyre, even as the forest is:
What if my leaves are falling like its own!
The tumult of thy mighty harmonies

Will take from both a deep, autumnal tone,
Sweet though in sadness.   Be thou, Spirit fierce,
My spirit!   Be thou me, impetuous one!

Drive my dead thoughts over the universe
Like withered leaves to quicken a new birth!
And, by the incantation of this verse,

Scatter, as from an unextinguished hearth
Ashes and sparks, my words among mankind!
Be through my lips to unawakened earth

The trumpet of a prophecy!   O Wind,
If Winter comes, can Spring be far behind?

PERCY BYSSHE SHELLEY.

Exercise 2[1]

(Reading time: about 6 minutes)

Color in everything!   From costly architecture down to 10-cent thimbles!

How did this great color movement start?

How far-reaching will it be?

How, when, and where will it end?

What effect is it having upon us?

How costly is it proving—to the manufacturer and to the consumer?

Should those who have not as yet applied color to their products do so, or is the movement almost over?

Answering the first question first, it does not so much matter how the movement originated.   Suffice to say it is here, and has almost completely engulfed us.   Some of those interviewed say that it came on us overnight.   Others, that it is a culmination of events, experiments, and education of the masses by manufacturers and others who desired to stimulate trade, and that it has gathered momentum gradually over a considerable period of time.

A noted psychologist attributes its origin to the great World War.   Color, he says, livens the senses, and keeps the individual alert to action.   It does not give the mind a chance to brood. Another authority links color with light and nature—we are more carefree and happy, more active, in a setting of nature in her most beautiful dress of sunlight and bright colors.

[1] HALL, HERBERT C., "Color—Is It a Fad," *The Magazine of Business* September, 1928.

The art director of a large concern lays the responsibility to the advent of the radio—of music and sound and animation. Color, according to him, is music to our eyes.

An official of a large western department store expresses the belief that in a measure the present broad use of color began with the Industrial Exposition in Paris in 1925. "It seems to have been about that time," says this merchandise authority, "that artists and artisans began to realize that people were tired of dull, meaningless, inarticulate backgrounds."

Be all this as it may, psychologists agree that color is as essential to our welfare as food and drink. They are equally unanimous that color is here to stay, perhaps not in the present-day extremes, but with some modification.

This last fact is of particular interest to manufacturers, who are vitally interested in its relation to their products. To them it is not an academic consideration, but a practical problem that must be met. The big question is, how shall they meet it?

Color has not yet been organized, and it is doubtful if it can be, unless or until there can be arranged a meeting of minds on the part of the majority. There is as yet no general movement on the part of manufacturers to standardize on colors, and yet, the vital need for such a movement has been recognized.

Take, for example, the Evanston, Illinois, society matron who desired to have her kitchen appointed in robin's egg blue. She went to a considerable expense in having imported Dutch ceramic tile set-in in her walls. She was able to get the proper shade of floor covering without much difficulty. But the best she could do in a kitchen cabinet and tables and chairs to match, was an off-shade blue. She reported that the plumbing fixtures were an "impossible blue which did not at all fit in with my color scheme." And the gas range was still another shade. She gave up her idea when she found it was utterly impossible to get cooking utensils to match the blue she so much wanted.

This woman, being quite wealthy as well as prominent, kept several manufacturers on the jump trying to satisfy her color whim. One manufacturer complained that she had thrown production in his plant off for nearly a week, and that he could not possibly hope to recover his loss.

It may be that the solution to these manufacturers' problems, as well as an idea of what others may expect to get into, will be found in one authority's opinion, which, in general, is shared by others: He says:

Color is here to stay as a primary factor in our living. Women are keenly interested in learning how to handle color effectively in dress, home decoration, and table decoration. But color to be an effective instrument in merchandising must be practical as well as artistic. A manufacturer must relate color in his product to the color developments in other products. The kitchen cabinet manufacturer, for instance, must offer his units in color treatments which will harmonize with current tendencies in wall coverings, draperies, floor materials, and so on.

Mass production and cheapness today are not enough. Our products must be really beautiful, and color is an important element. We must remember that the public taste is being rapidly educated to an appreciation of what is really good. The philosophers long ago pointed out the influence of beauty on higher ethical standards. Beauty in our surroundings, homes, our dress, reflects itself in an urge towards beauty in the art of living.

In the Old World beauty is limited to the few, but in the New World we have increasing general prosperity, coupled with the fact that mass production does make available to the masses articles that are intrinsically artistic in design and color. As a result, beauty is now within the reach of the many.

Applied psychology teaches us that color has an absolute and definite bearing on our reactions. As people become more and more skilled in the effective use of color in their surroundings, better standards of living will naturally follow.

Referring to the problem of relating the colors of products in various lines, another authority declares that there is a great need for some sort of color standardization. He refers to the success achieved in the textile industry through the development of the Textile Color Card Association. In advance of each season, color trends are studied by this association and forecasts made. This permits the shoe manufacturers, the hosiery manufacturers, the dress manufacturers, the millinery manufacturers— and all the other factors in the garment and allied trades—to plan their offerings so that ultimately a woman is able to buy an ensemble that will harmonize.

The forecasts of this association are studied by the manufacturers in many lines—from handkerchiefs to motor cars. The result is the elimination of a great deal of the risk and expense formerly involved.

With the consumer, color may be a whim; but to the producer it can be disastrous. The experience of a large manufacturer of quality gas and coal ranges has proved not only costly, but manufacturing complications have arisen to such an extent that the company is now seeking immediate relief.

Color is proving a nightmare with us, this manufacturer states.

We have become involved in tremendous manufacturing costs that we could not possibly have included in our original estimate, when we decided to bow to what we thought was the popular demand for our product in color.

And we can never expect to recover. The public—I am now talking about the majority of consumer prospects—admires our product in color, yes; but when it finds the cost to be somewhat higher than our ranges in plain black and white, or black and gray, it invariably buys the plain ones. And yet, color is just enough in demand to make it necessary for us to continue it.

White or gray opaque that is so commonly used in our white or gray enamel backs, legs, and bases, costs 50 cents a pound. Certain colored opaques which are necessary to obtain a range of colors in our enamels cost from $4 to $6 a pound. This brings the cost of our colored ranges up more than 15 per cent—oftentimes as high as 25 per cent.

We must also include in that increased cost our increased production costs. Production is slowed down considerably by color. We are dealing with an uncertain element in colored enamels. It is almost impossible to match colors successfully in different runs. We may be able to get a delicate blue today—tomorrow, in trying to mix the same color, we will get a harsher blue. Hours are spent in trying to get as nearly a perfect match as possible, for it would not do to have different shades of the same color on display on a dealer's floor.

Distribution also suffers. Certain colors may prove popular in certain localities; other colors, in other localities. We have found it necessary to incur tremendously heavy traffic costs in switching our ranges around from one dealer in one town, to another in a distant one.

Blue may now be popular in Chicago, and green in New York. Ivory may sell more rapidly in Detroit, and olive in Pittsburgh. It cost thousands of dollars to determine this, and tomorrow it may all be changed.

There has not been any move that we know of on the part of range and furnace manufacturers—yes, eventually, I am afraid that we will have to get into the manufacture of furnaces in color—to standardize on colors. We are seriously thinking of taking the initiative to see if this cannot be done. I should say that standardization on three colors would prove to be the most practical.

Unless something is done, and done quickly, I fear for the health of our industry. Manufacturers are bringing color abuses upon themselves. I do not believe that color is exactly a fad, but I also do not believe that we will continue to have such a wide range of choice. Business cannot stand it, that is all.

Another stove and range manufacturer has compromised with the "color fad" by introducing color into only certain parts of his ranges, so that they will have a color effect without being in full color. These parts are easily interchangeable, so that the problem of suiting localities or meeting special consumers' tastes is greatly simplified. This idea might be adapted to other products. This manufacturer admits, however, that these partially colored ranges do not sell as readily as the fully colored ones.

Range and furnace manufacturers, as well as other manufacturers who are similarly hard hit, may find consolation in the opinion of the vice-president of a large varnish manufacturing company, who faces the color problem every minute of the day.

It is my opinion that color is still in the ascendency but that its popularity will have a tendency to kill itself to a certain extent.

The development in the use of color seems to have resulted in a regular spree, bringing unlooked for manufacturing difficulties in certain lines of industry. In any case, what looked like a pretty sales proposition brought untold difficulties in production and distribution.

I believe the trend of less color in manufactured articles will be noticeable as soon as the burden of production becomes too great.

There must be a happy medium between the regular old black model T Ford and the special paint job, or a different optional color scheme for every car manufactured. What that is will be determined largely by the price the public is willing to pay for color.

I do believe this color orgy is a fine thing for the public and will result in a better understanding of color in general, and I further believe that when the storm blows over there will not be so much color as there is at present, but more than there was.

Color is "coming in strong" in men's clothes—color and a corresponding accentuation in weave. Upon being shown the weave of an advance pattern for the new season, one is apt to remark, "Is that not rather futuristic?"

Exercise 3[1]

AVERAGE READING

(Reading rate: four words per second)
(Reading time: about 2 minutes)

The keynote of Mr. Hoover's program is individual opportunity as opposed to an unnecessary governmental interference. It is that purpose which runs through all the planning of his ingenious mind. He is seeking not to aggrandize the Government, but the individual; to give him a better chance and a freer life; to make Government his servant, not his master. He believes our Government to be founded upon "the conception that only through ordered liberty, freedom and equal opportunity to the individual will his initiative and enterprise spur on the march of progress. And in our insistence upon equality of opportunity has our system advanced beyond all the world." These are not the mere words or the pleasing generalities of a politician. With Mr. Hoover they are the very essence of practical proposals. It is in this view that Herbert Hoover is absolutely opposed to the unwarrantable extension of bureaucratic government. Again let him voice his convictions:

"Every step of bureaucratizing of the business of our country poisons the very roots of liberalism. That is, political equality, free speech, free assembly, free press, and equality of opportunity. It is the road not to more liberty, but to less liberty.

[1] New York *Times*.

Liberalism should be found not striving to spread bureaucracy but striving to set bounds to it. True liberalism seeks all legitimate freedom fired in the confident belief that without such freedom the pursuit of all other blessings and benefits is vain. That belief is the foundation of all American progress, political and economic."

Herbert Hoover finds no inconsistency in conserving our natural resources, in maintaining the control essential to protect the public interest, with the opposition to any unnecessary extension of bureaucratic administration. Let him again speak: "It does not mean that our Government is to part with one iota of its national resources without complete protection of the public interests." He believes in a system of regulation which will conserve both the public interest and the opportunity for fair individual enterprises. He points out that the Republican Administration has "insisted upon the principle that when great public utilities were clothed with the security of partial monopoly, whether it be railways, power plants, telephones or what not, then there must be the fullest and most complete control of rates, services and finances by Government or local agencies.

It is in the light of the necessity of conserving the freedom of honest enterprise that Mr. Hoover deals with the fundamental needs of labor. You cannot protect labor by facilitating strife or by merely laying down rules for the efficient conduct of labor wars. The real protection of labor is in continuous employment and in the conditions of production, distribution and exchange at good wages. The key to labor's door of hope is employment, the maintenance of a vast purchasing power which makes production possible.

Exercise 4[1]

(Reading time: about 2 minutes)

It is natural to believe in great men. If the companions of our childhood should turn out to be heroes, and their condition regal, it would not suprise us. All mythology opens with demi-

[1] EMERSON, RALPH WALDO, "Great Men."

gods, and the circumstance is high and poetic; that is, their genius is paramount. In the legends of the Gautama, the first men ate the earth, and found it deliciously sweet.

Nature seems to exist for the excellent. The world is upheld by the veracity of good men: they make the earth wholesome. They who lived with them found life glad and nutritious. Life is sweet and tolerable only in our belief in such society; and actually, or ideally, we manage to live with superiors. We call our children and our lands by their names. Their names are wrought into the verbs of language, their works and effigies are in our houses, and every circumstance of the day recalls an anecdote of them.

The search after the great is the dream of youth, and the most serious occupation of manhood. We travel into foreign parts to find his works,—if possible, to get a glimpse of him. But we are put off with fortune instead. You say, the English are practical; the Germans are hospitable; in Valencia, the climate is delicious; and in the hills of the Sacramento, there is gold for the gathering. Yes, but I do not travel to find comfortable, rich, and hospitable people, or clear sky, or ingots that cost too much. But if there were any magnet that would point to the countries and houses where are the persons who are intrinsically rich and powerful, I would sell all, and buy it and put myself on the road today.

The race goes with us on their credit. The knowledge, that in the city is a man who invented the railroad, raises the credit of all the citizens. But enormous populations, if they be beggars, are disgusting, like moving cheese, like hills of ants, or of fleas—the more, the worse.

Our religion is the love and cherishing of these patrons. The gods of fable are the shining moments of great men. We run all our vessels into one mould. Our colossal theologies of Judaism, Christism, Buddhism, Mahometism, are the necessary and structural action of the human mind. The student of history is like a man going into a warehouse to buy cloths or carpets. He fancies he has a new article. If he go to the factory, he shall find that his new stuff still repeats the scrolls and rosettes which are found on the interior walls of the pyramids of Thebes.

Our theism is the purification of the human mind. Man can paint, or make, or think nothing but man. He believes that the great material elements had their origin from his thought. And our philosophy finds one essence collected or distributed.

Exercise 5[1]

(Reading time: about 6 minutes)

Since the sixteenth century courts of law have told man, *Cujus est solus, ejus est usque ad coelum.* This, being freely translated, declares that he who owns the soil owns all the way to Heaven. Apparently, man has decided to improve all of this, his property, instead of only part of it as heretofore.

If we are to believe the principal architects and builders of the country, the upward ascent has only begun. Just so long as taller structures can be made to show a profit and not add too much of congestion to streets increasingly used, tall and yet taller structures will be built.

Yesterday's sky-line has receded as far as mutton-leg sleeves, the hitching-post, cherry phosphate, and peg-top trousers. To-day's sky-line is dipped in magic; tomorrow's will exceed the liveliest imaginations, of that we are sure.

The builder is now exercising in part the dominion he has given over all the earth, and he is building everywhere in the cities offices and homes pointed directly skyward.

Tall buildings are born of the herding of men into preferred areas, and of the increase in land values and consequent high taxes. As the demand for space in which to live and work has increased, the ground area remaining constant, the cities have taken to the air. The "great open spaces" are now from 30 to 40 floors up.

Probably the Grand Central development in New York has attracted more attention than any group of building projects, and with good reason. Here building construction started from the rock up; here first use was made of "air rights," a subject that vastly intrigues American business men today. Those

[1] BURRITT, RICHARD C., "From the Ground Up," *Magazine of Business*, July, 1928.

developed in connection with the Grand Central center in New York have added a staggering sum to the income of the New York Central Railroad.

The Grand Central development is an interesting one. A station that occupied part of the site where now stands the Municipal Building, in 1839, provided New York City with its first railroad passenger terminal. Subsequently the station moved northward, keeping step with the march of population.

It was Commodore Vanderbilt who selected the Grand Central site on Forty-second Street. He moved to name the station "Grand Central" because of the accessibility of its location.

On Commodore Vanderbilt's site, the New York Central, in 1903, started the preliminary work on the present Grand Central Station project. Plans were perfected for two-level yard underground, for electrification and reclamation of all the space over the tracks.

Two miles of city streets were opened and forty acres of air-rights were made available for building purposes.

The new enlarged depot opened in 1913. By that time several great structures had been reared on air-rights, and the area is now filled with large buildings.

Officials planned the Grand Central Station capacity to be equal to all demands that might be placed upon it for many years to come. But they could not visualize the great army of commuters that would be flowing through in another decade. The station is not yet swamped. The efficiency and speed with which its functions are performed, obviate that. Yet it is only a question of time before new facilities will be required.

Meanwhile, the further development of the Grand Central zone "from the ground up," goes on. A great office building is under construction directly behind the Grand Central Terminal Building. This new building, to be known as the New York Central Building, is one of the most interesting building projects in the country—interesting because of the fact that it is not only built on air-rights, but also because it will span Park Avenue and vehicular traffic will flow through it on ramp roadways, rising from the street level at Forty-sixth Street, passing above Forty-fifth Street, and thence on around the terminal building.

The building will tower 35 stories above the street—a startling fact in itself when it is recalled that when the Grand Central Terminal was built its developers agreed that six stories would probably be the limit of construction on air-rights!

It is interesting to know that the air-rights in the Grand Central zone are held by the terminal company and leases are made for 21 years, with two options to renew, in short providing for a term lease of 63 years.

But the attention accorded Manhattan recently has been diverted to Chicago. Two undertakings predicated upon air-rights bring Chicago prominently forward in any report of current progress on building from the ground up.

These are the Chicago Merchandise Mart to be erected by Marshall Field and Company at the riverside not far from the present site of the Chicago and North Western Railway passenger station. And the *Chicago Daily News* building, which is at present in process of construction at the riverside within a few blocks, and immediately east of the railway station.

Announced to cost $30,000,000, the Merchandise Mart will be twice the size of the world's largest business building, now the Furniture Mart, another Chicago structure with a commanding position near the Municipal Pier.

The Merchandise Mart will have a total floor space of 4,000,000 square feet. It will rise 18 to 23 stories in height and will house a concentration of manufacturer's exhibits from which retail merchants may make their selections of the world's merchandise, all under one roof.

A multiplicity of items might be recorded as to what this mart will include. But none of them would prove more engaging than a statement of what has been purchased for the building in land and air-rights.

Straight down the center of the property lies a strip bought outright. On either side of it the map makers have checked off 375 parcels of ground, each nine feet in diameter. Each separate parcel is owned by Marshall Field and Company in fee. Each was purchased that the company might own the ground in which will be placed the caissons upon which the supporting columns of the building will rest.

The supporting columns will be prismatic in shape. The space they occupy has been purchased—an additional 375 parcels.

The building proper will occupy an air-lot which will rise from a plane 23 feet above river datum.

Frederick Hack, attorney for the company, and Herbert Becker, vice-president of the Chicago Title and Trust Company, devised the lot system involved, which sets a precedent in the acquisition of air-rights. They explain that it was necessary for Marshall Field and Company to take title because the railway property is subject to a general refunding mortgage.

As Mr. Becker explained, Marshall Field and Company subdivided land and air horizontally and vertically to perfect its title to the property required.

A short distance to the south, at the Madison Street bridge and directly across the Chicago River from the site where the Chicago Civic Opera Company's 40-story skyscraper is to be erected, *The Chicago Daily News* is exercising air-rights in the building of a new plant and office building. This structure, 26 stories in height, will rest upon piers set on caissons placed on bed-rock 100 feet below the surface of the ground. Bed-rock in Chicago's loop area is that deep beneath the surface, or even deeper.

A lease for 99 years is held on the air-rights involved and one strip on either side is owned in fee. The railway tracks at one point are so close together that only a few columns can be dropped among them. The solution is to employ cantilevers, girders, and trusses. The piers are regularly spaced, however, on the strips owned in fee.

According to Laird Bell, counsel for *The Chicago Daily News*, this lease has much in common with leases that have been executed in eastern states. Unlike Marshall Field and Company, however, the newspaper did not specify and then purchase the parcels in which the caissons are placed, but retained the right, subject to the consent of the Union Station Company, to drop as many piers as would be necessary for proper construction and these parcels, once agreed upon and then placed in use, then come under the terms of the contract.

Railway locomotive equipment passing beneath this building is not electrified, wherefore an effective arrangement had to be devised for smoke abatement. It will be done on this wise: Smoke from the locomotives will pass through orifices into a horizontal chamber connecting with a stack 400 feet square and extending upward through the center of the building. Thus the railroad will smoke through a chimney extending up through the air-rights it has leased.

One feature of this newspaper building is significant of the time. A private roadway broad enough to permit trucks to pass each other and widening considerably in the center of the building to allow for loading and unloading facilities, will be built from the street floor through the midsection of the building.

Approval by the Illinois Commerce Commission of *The Chicago Daily News* air-rights lease paved the way for development of enormous holdings in the Chicago district.

Before dismissing the subject of air-rights in Chicago, attention must be drawn to the Illinois Central Railroad, with tracks extending along Chicago's lake front from the Chicago River on the north to the far South Side. Potentially this railroad has one of the richest holdings known. These are air-rights that Charles Markham, chairman of the board, estimated as worth $100,000000. Many consider that figure a mere fraction of the potential value of these rights.

SOLID READING

(Reading rate: three words per second)

Exercise 6[1]

(Reading time: about 8 minutes)

As you drive along Route No. 10, two miles west of Champaign, Illinois, you see in the corner of a corn-field this sign:

THE VAN WEGEN FARM
Operated by a
Business System

[1] MILLAR, JOHN H., "After All Isn't Farming a Business," *Magazine of Business*, November, 1928.

This is one of 32 farms, totaling 7,500 acres, operated by the Farm Management Department—which is Joseph E. Johnson—of the Citizens' State Bank of Champaign, a $3,500,000 institution. Mr. Johnson, himself a farm owner and a scientifically trained farmer, was for 10 years a country banker and elevator operator in a small town in Champaign County, then for four years business manager of the Champaign County Farm Bureau, the position he left on March 2, 1925, to take up his present work.

The bank pays Mr. Johnson a salary and bonus, and charges the land-owners $1 a year per acre for his services. There is no new relationship between farm owner and tenant. The bank's farm manager simply acts as the agent of the owner, just as the officer of a corporation acts as the agent of the stockholders. Capital, labor, and management are definitely separated in the same way as is almost universally the practice in other lines of industry.

This Farm Management Department is not makeshift arrangement for handling land forced into the bank's possession. On the contrary, none of the farms belong to the bank. They are the property of owners, who have had difficulty getting satisfactory tenants or who have experienced other troubles connected with land ownership, and have come of their own free will to ask the bank to take charge of their farms for them. No attempt is made to seek new bank accounts through the department; tenants and landlords are told that they are at liberty to deposit their money anywhere they please. The largest farm on the list belongs to the head of a competing bank.

Two waiting lists are on file in the Champaign State Bank. One is of farms whose owners want the bank to take them over, the other is a list of tenants seeking places on a Johnson-managed farm.

Unless owners are willing to put back into their farms enough of their income to build up steadily the fertility of the soil and keep the improvements in good shape, their land will not be taken. Mr. Johnson uses paint freely.

In selecting tenants, care is taken to see that each man is placed on a farm of the size and type of agriculture for which he and his family are best suited. Mr. Johnson believes that farm‑ ing is 25 per cent farm and 75 per cent farmer, and that the first and most important qualification of the farm operator is willingness to work hard and keep on doing it. Some of the best results have been achieved with industrious tenants whose previous experience in farming had been limited. They have nothing to unlearn, they do as they are told.

A. M. Burke, himself the owner of four farms, president of the bank, sat at his desk on a Saturday morning in September, telling why he started this Farm Management Department over three years ago, and what results could be expected when a farm is "operated by a business system." For half an hour he talked about farms and farming without once mentioning "farm relief" —a record yet to be made by any politician.

What Congress may or may not do for agriculture in the com‑ ing session did not seem to concern Mr. Burke.

One farmer after another came into the bank, he greeted them all by their first names. As one of them walked out, he remarked,

"See that man going out the door over there? Well, we handle $30,000 or $40,000 of his investments back in our collection department. The other day he bought a small farm and paid cash for it. He doesn't seem to have any trouble making money out of farming. And I don't suppose there is a month goes by that he doesn't come in here and talk over some problem of his with Johnson. The farmers who bank here are always after Johnson; there are four or five of them back there talking to him right now; the only way he can get away from them is to leave the bank and not tell anyone where he is going."

And then Mr. Burke added, "Any man who knows something about farming, and is really willing to work steadily, can make money on a farm if he is not too much in debt." Obviously Mr. Burke was not running for a political office. He is just a banker‑ farmer talking about the business that is his life work.

Political campaigns during the past year have brought forth such extended and heated discussions of farm ailments and plans for curing them that it is difficult for business men not to get the impression that agriculture is marking time waiting for Congress and the new President to decide what is to be done to save the day.

Quite the contrary is the case. Agriculture is on the move, it is changing, and changing rapidly. Since 1919, our farm population has decreased 3,000,000; there are now several million less acres under cultivation. And yet our crops in recent years have been somewhat larger than they were before the war. Production per man and production per acre have both been climbing. In spite of the farmers' shortage of money tractors in use increased from 246,000 on January 1, 1920, to 506,000 on January 1, 1925. Agriculture is steadily becoming more efficient.

When the present acute situation is a thing of the past, and we can look back and see how relief actually was brought about, the chances are we will discover that the one most effective force was the farmer himself, who year after year increased his own and his soil's efficiency through the application to farming of scientific knowledge and business management. As Mr. Johnson expressed it:

If we ever get any permanent, workable improvement in agriculture, it is going to be brought about by the use of business methods in farming, and by the coöperation of the business interests of the country with the farmer. There is no conflict between business and agriculture their problems are the same; so must their methods be, also.

But how much does "operated by a business system" mean to a farm in actual dollars?

Some significant figures are available. Out in western Illinois, between Galesburg and Moline, lies Henry County, a rich general farming community in which the livestock industry is highly developed. In 1927 sixty farmers, scattered over the county, kept books of account of their operations, following a standard system worked out by the Department of Farm Organization and Management of the University of Illinois College of Agriculture. At the end of the year their books were sent to the college to be audited. To begin with it was found, as might be expected, that the 60 farmers businesslike enough to keep exact accounts, made somewhat more money than those who did not. They ran about $1,000 above the average farm income of the county.

But far more significant was the variation between the 60 farms. These were ranked according to money made, and then the average earnings of the first third compared with the average earnings of the last third. It was not the best against the poorest, but the average of the 20 best against the average of the 20 poorest.

It was found, after charging off all expenses of operation and allowing 5 per cent interest on the total investment in land, buildings, equipment, and live stock ($55,432 each for the 20 best farms, averaging 229.3 acres; $45,866 each for the 20 poorest, averaging 200.1 acres), that the 20 most profitable farms had earned an average of $1,997 each to pay the farmer for his personal labor, unpaid family labor, management, and risk; while the 20 least profitable not only had earned nothing, but lacked $1,074 each of making the 5 per cent interest charges. There was therefore a difference in earnings of $3,071 per farm between the best third and the poorest third.

Since about the same variation has been found in other communities where similar audits have been made, it is safe to conclude that, in the heart of the corn belt, good farmers on 200-acre farms of diversified agriculture are about $3,000 a year better off than mediocre ones, and about $4,000 a year better off than the really poor ones who keep no accounts. To quote Mr. Johnson again, "Farming is 25 per cent farm, and 75 per cent farmer."

But the College of Agriculture went into the figures still further and accounted for some $2,000 of the $3,000 difference by the following five factors—all, it will be noted, are management factors:

Crop yields.. ...	$735
Kinds of crops....................................	146
Efficiency of live stock............................	625
Efficiency of power and machinery...................	269
Efficiency of man labor............................	215

That the better managers would be likely to use better judgment in marketing and take more care to avoid expense leaks would account for a good portion of the remaining $1,000 difference. Summing it up in one word, the cause of the $3,000 difference is—management.

We see, therefore, how large may be the earnings of the 32 owners who are paying the Champaign State Bank $7,500 a year to provide this essential scientific business management. If Mr. Johnson is as good a manager as an ordinary good farmer, the expectation is that the income from the 32 farms under his management will be $96,000 a year more than if the same farms were run by mediocre tenants. However, since he has already demonstrated that he can get crop yields and cash returns somewhat greater than the average of the 20 best farmers in that Henry County group, the expectation of increased income from farms under his management is still larger.

It is interesting to observe just how a scientific farm manager gets his results. Take, for example, the invisible load of hay to which are hitched the horses seen in the background of the picture of Mr. Johnson and one of his farm operators. It is soybean hay from a certain 40-acre field on the Van Wegen farm.

Exercise 7[1]

(Reading time: about 8 minutes)

There are five things which constitute mental training, and the man who can do these five things, no matter where he has learned them or how he has learned them, is a trained thinker.

1. Can he recognize a fact?
2. Can he make a distinction?
3. Can he draw an inference?
4. Can he judge evidence?
5. Can he concentrate his attention?

No special subject-matter is required as a means of developing ability along any one of these lines. You do not have to study Latin or mathematics in order to train your mind in any one of these essentials. If you are a mathematician, then you must learn to recognize mathematical facts, to draw mathemati

---

[1] McClure, M. T., "How To Think in Business," McGraw-Hill Book Company, Inc., 1923.

cal inferences, to make mathematical distinctions, to judge mathematical evidence, and to do each of these with concentrated effort. And if you are a business man, what you must do in a sustained way is to see business facts, deal with business distinctions and inferences, and estimate business evidence. All of the subject-matter you need for training you have at your disposal.

Thinking is a natural thing, just as natural as breathing or nutrition. This means that one does not learn to think any more than he learns to breathe or to assimilate food. No one can *learn* to live, he can only learn to live *well*. The same is true of thinking. You do not learn to think; what you learn to do is to *improve* your thinking.

Training in the ability to do clear thinking is primarily a matter of improving your methods of handling the difficulties that confront you. Intelligence is not a thing; the word rather stands for effective and successful mental activity. The training of the mind consists in the formation of accurate and careful habits to replace the more or less crude and careless blunderings of unsystematic thinking. It consists in improving the *ways* and *methods* of doing the things that make up the routine of daily life. Few of you can change your occupation; what you can do is to bring increased efficiency into what you are already doing. Mental training means the gradual and steady building up of a scientific method of procedure to be used in place of the unregulated method of chance guessing, luck and accident.

Let us dispel at once a prevailing mystery that attaches to the word "scientific." There is the widespread feeling that the scientist uses thought processes that are unfamiliar and inaccessible to common, ordinary people. There is the feeling that he uses a method that the rest of us can not use and that he exercises functions that we can not understand. That is not so. The scientist can do nothing different in kind from what we do. All that he can do is to observe facts, make distinctions, draw inferences, and pass judgments. He is superior to us in that in a sustained effort he observes more clearly, infers more safely and judges more soundly. There is no difference in kind between the thought processes involved in looking for your hat when you have lost it and the thought processes involved in the scientific discovery of an element or in the working out along scientific lines of a policy for the internationalization of banking. Science differs from common sense in method, and in method alone.

The untrained mind proceeds in a hop-skip-and-jump sort of way. There is much of hit or miss in its actions, with the probability of more misses than hits. This is termed the "trial and error" method. We simply do something, and when that fails we do something else, and keep on trying until we hit on something which works. It is surprising how much in our lives we leave to accident. Men dislike to assume responsibility. They would rather take a chance and drift. Wundt was probably right when he said that animals think never and men but seldom. And when they do think, about the last thing they think about is thinking. Emerson said of Napoleon: "He never blundered into a victory. He gained his battles in his head before he won them in the field."

Scientific method means that the thought process is regulated and controlled. It means the formation of alert, accurate, and careful mental habits. The scientist is a trained observer. His method differs from the ordinary method of unsystematic thinking in that it is more precise, thorough, definite, exact, and accurate. He is more *thoughtful*. Practically, that means that he pays more attention to his problem; that he takes pains in trying to solve it; he gives his mind to it. That is, he weighs his difficulty, deliberates about it, examines it, turns it over in order to look at it from different angles, and to see it in different lights. Like the mathematician, he calculates in order to be definite, and like the physicist, he weighs in order to be accurate. When we say that he is methodical we mean that he is orderly.

It should be borne in mind that what we shall herein describe under the caption of reflective thinking is to be identified with what is generally termed the scientific method in thinking. In short, mind is method. To know is, on its practical side at least, *to know how*. A description of the "how" of business procedure is a description of business intelligence. Business is largely concerned with ways of doing things, and progress in business is concerned with better ways of doing them. A glance at such a magazine as *SYSTEM*, a magazine devoted to the upbuilding of business morale and to the development of practical business intelligence, will serve to illustrate the point. An examination of the table of contents shows the recurrence of such titles as "Better Ways to Manage," "Seven Plans that Save," "Timely Buying Ideas," "How Our Customers Merchandize for Us," "How to Train a General Manager," "How We Keep Finding a New Way to Save," etc. What is described under these titles is a way of doing things, a method of procedure. Little is said of intelligence as such, but much is said about form and technique, about practical adaptation of new plans, about ways to revise, to recognize, to reshape. One man finds that a plan of procedure, or a policy of administration, or some guiding idea or principle has proved effective in practice and he describes its mode of operation in the hope that it may be of use to some one else. A description of the technique of business reconstruction *is* a description of business intelligence.

It is necessary to enter a certain caution in regard to the subject of method. You do not first acquire a method and then proceed to use it. You can not reach the final point of a highly trained mind by trying to impose the finished technique on a beginner. The gap between the trained and the untrained mind cannot be bridged by super-imposing a highly specialized technique at the start. You begin by doing a thing in a crude way, and by repetition and effort you gradually improve your method. You must first do something before you can do it well.

What is of importance is that you actually handle problems that involve thinking as a means to their solution. The danger in training of method is that "we hang our clothes on a hickory limb, and don't go near the water." One learns to swim by swimming. You learn to think by thinking. In cultivating the power of thinking, it is essential that you actually deal with difficulties. Your major aim is not to learn to think, but to learn to solve problems; thinking is a means to this end.

Perfection of method comes gradually through practice. We acquire skill in thinking in the same way that we acquire skill in any other activity, namely, by performing that activity. You may know all that there is to know about baseball from the standpoint of a spectator who sits in the grandstand. But that information would never enable you to go on to the field and play a winning game. To know *about* the game is one thing; to be able to play the game is another thing. In accordance with what we have stated to be the aim of this book, the training of mind does not consist in acquiring knowledge about thinking, it consists in the making of one into a thoughtful person. Skill comes with practice. You do not learn in moments of resolve, you learn only as you put into operation the resolutions you form. Thinking *about* courage will never make a man courageous. He becomes courageous by *doing* courageous things. Assume, then, an active attitude of mind. Accept every opportunity that lends itself to reflection, for only by actual contact with problems will you ever acquire a method of solving them.

It may be added that there is no *one* best way. Each must work out for himself the method that is best suited to his own special type of difficulty.

Success in life depends on ability to solve the problems that arise in the course of daily experience. Thinking is a means to this end. Training in mental power resolves itself into the concrete task of acquiring an effective method of overcoming difficulties. It is the aim of this book to present the essential features of scientific method in their relation to the actual and concrete problems of business experience.

Exercise 8[1]

(Reading time: about 8 minutes)

The truly prodigious economic advance that has been achieved in the United States since the war has puzzled and astounded the rest of the world, and we ourselves have been rather bewildered by it. To many embittered, and more or less chronic cynics on both sides of the Atlantic, to whom anything concerned with the "march of materialism" in America is but a doleful soul-destroying clatter, the past decade has enthroned the Moloch of machinery even higher and ground the "wage slaves" even lower.

[1] KLEIN, JULIUS, "Serving our 260 American Wage," *Magazine of Business*, July, 1928.

In such circumstances any talk of better living is, to their thinking, rather ghastly humor.

Just what is the result of this newer machine age in terms of the outlook for the worker? Is it really but the ruthless domination of steel over the minds and souls of men?

Almost daily we read the announcements of the latest triumph of some inventive genius whereby the power of electricity or steam has again been harnessed to lift yet another age-old burden from the sweating backs of the toilers. For this relief, much thanks, says the humanitarian. But the wage-earner, who must live by that sweat, may not be quite so satisfied. What about his job? He is grateful, of course, to have had it made easier; but to wipe it out entirely with one stroke of a machine piston, so to speak, is "something else again."

In other words, the question is: Does our much vaunted efficiency, which has been the wonder of the world and the pet theme of our patrioteering orators, make for a good standard of living? Does it not, in fact, actually endanger any kind of living for the worker in many cases?

There can be no doubt of the onward march of the machine and of its displacement of artisans in almost every craft. Scarcely an industry has escaped the "mass mania," the consuming thirst for volume and yet more volume of production, which, incidentally, is not always synonymous with profit. The output per worker in our manufacturing industries has nearly doubled in the last generation. If one man now does the work of two, what happens to that other man? Is it any consolation to him that his place has been taken by a clattering, soulless "robot," whose daily fodder is merely a few ounces of oil or throbs of electricity?

A great automobile company increases its production 1,400 per cent with an addition of only 10 per cent to its personnel. In automotive manufacturing as a whole the actual output per worker has risen from 7.2 units (cars, trucks, and so on) in 1913 to 11.5 at present. In other words, the need for labor in the industry has decreased more than 50 per cent in ratio to the production.

In the presence of these figures and of those on the other side of the ledger, namely, the totals of unemployed, which, though slightly above those of a year ago, are happily decreasing, why question this ominous aspect of the spread of "efficiency" of our labor-saving devices?   Why doubt this sinister menace to the job holder?

Such reasoning, though superficially logical, overlooks one vital factor in the whole of this postwar economic development. With the onward sweep of machinery there has come a steadily upward trend of wages for the machine operator, and consequently of buying power.   Ordinarily, such a stimulus of demand would promptly boost prices, but mass production made possible by the new mechanical equipment has kept them down.

Incidentally, this mounting wage scale of ours has by no means crippled our competitive powers as against our European rivals in neutral markets.   Taking the 1913 figures as a 100 index, wages paid in the United States in 1927 stood at 260, while those in the United Kingdom were 180, but the price-levels in the two countries were 145 and 142, respectively.   Our wage scale had gone up more than 40 per cent beyond the British but prices and living costs in the two countries had kept side by side.

Those figures tell the tale.   It is the extra buying power in the 260 American wage which gives our worker the added margin of purchasing ability that has been translated into our new standard of *comfortable* living.   The ratio of buying command of the American 260 over our 145 price-level as compared with the British 180 over its 142 price-index sums up the whole philosophy of present-day American prosperity.

That, objects the doleful cynic, may be satisfactory for the worker who held his job and is operating the machine, but what becomes of his displaced shop-mate?   Where does he figure in the advancing wage scale?

The answer is that while he has lost one job in a factory he has open to him another in a non-manufacturing service industry, which has grown up as a result of this rising comfort level demanded by his former associate because of the latter's new wages.

This is by no means intended to imply that the widespread readjustments incident to the spread of machinery have been entirely devoid of hardships.   Far from it.   Every such turning point in economic history since the earliest days of the first applications of primitive devices to aid the work of hands and arms has involved some temporary hardships as the change was being affected. The industrial development of England during the seventeenth and eighteenth centuries was punctuated with violent outbursts by the workers who feared displacement by the progress of machinery, particularly in the textile and iron industries.

But out of it all—and indeed rather promptly—there emerged a new standard of living which England had never known before. The records of the early factories are smeared with ghastly tales of the sufferings of women and child workers, of ruthless employer autocracy, and of the pitiless exploitation. The grim horrors of these phases cannot be ignored. But by their very striking dramatic picturesqueness, all too frequently they have obscured our appreciation of the fact that meanwhile there coursed through the people a new vigor, new aspirations, and with them the means for their gratification.

It was this stirring turmoil of social and economic discontent which gave birth to the elements of British democracy whence came the leadership that delivered Europe from the perils of Napoleonic despotism and finally reached its full stature in the reforms of 1832.

Had this industrial epic occurred just a generation earlier, one wonders whether there would have been that wide gulf between the standards of civil and economic liberty of the motherland and of the colonies in America which brought about the breach of 1776.

The beginning of the machine age, despite its temporary sordid aspects, lifted the people to newer heights of well-being previously unattained. The observations of many keen-eyed contemporaries reflected unmistakably this profoundly significant social upheaval, this suddenly achieved consciousness of better living and the possibilities of its attainment. As Sidney Webb so forcefully described this new era "the whole nation shared in the ever-growing stream of commodities and steadily widened the range and increased the quantity of its consumption."

And so today in America we are witnessing the development of these newer service industries as the inevitable accompaniment of our industrial advance. They are the expression of these same aspirations for greater comforts and for social betterment in its larger sense among our wage-earners as were manifested under such profoundly significant circumstances during the dramatic days of the industrial revolution.

Our factories have decreased their employees by 917,000 since 1920, partly as a normal deflation of military activities, but particularly because of the vastly improved production efficiency of the plants—better machinery, more experienced workers, and better shop management and executive direction.

The industrialization of agriculture is largely responsible for the fact that the employees of our farms have decreased by 800,000 since the war. Of course, there are other factors that enter into that situation, such as the falling off in the number of horses in the country from 21,500,000 to 15,300,000 since 1919.

Efficiency methods in locomotive construction, roundhouse operation, and freight servicing account for a good part of the 240,000 men released from the payrolls of our railways at that time.

If allowed to stand by themselves, these figures would present a dark aspect indeed. But they depict only a part of the situation. As indicated above, the increased wages earned by those workmen who have been retained in the factories and railways and on the farms have stirred a nation-wide demand for low-priced automobiles, for radios, for telephones, for motion-pictures, for cabarets, for restaurants, and for countless other contributions to comfort. These must not only be built; they must constantly be serviced.

The result is that over 760,000 men have found employ- ment since 1920 in driving and ministering to the automobile. Nearly 100,000 of these are chauffeurs of sightseeing cars and other types of busses. Perhaps the bus has slightly cut down the job prospects for locomotive engineers and trainmen, but new positions have promptly risen to fill the gap. This is an impressive index of the amazing increase in our automotive vehicles which has grown so rapidly that we have a car for every five persons in the country, so that in the event of some great national emergency the entire population could be bundled into automobiles and driven across the borders!

HEAVY READING

(Reading rate: 6,000 words per hour)

Exercise 9[1]

(Reading time: about 6 minutes)

. . . The Hertzian experiments . . . remind one of Franklin's Leyden-jar experiments; but Hertz, fully equipped with Maxwell's theory, employed a special form of a Leyden jar, which radiates more abundantly waves of Faraday's fluxes. It looks like a dumb-bell and consists of two spheres, A and B, with projecting rods C and D. A and C represent one conducting plate of the jar, B and D represent the other; the insulator between the two conducting plates was air. Let an electrical machine generate a positive charge on conductor AC, and a negative charge on conductor BD. The charges on these two conductors are interconnected by the electrical flux; the directions of the flux reactions at various points of space are indicated by the dotted curves . . . they form tubular surfaces, the cross-sections of which represent roughly the density of the electrical flux at various points. The symmetry of the apparatus makes it obvious that the distribution of the electrical flux must be symmetrical with respect to the axis of symmetry of the apparatus, that is the axis of the cylinders C and D. The energy of the electrical flux is located in the space covered by the dotted curves (diagram given) and distributed in a perfectly symmetrical manner. The release of this energy initiates the flux actions which are to be transmitted. This release occurs as follows: When the charge is sufficiently large, and, as a result, the electrical force between C and D is sufficiently high, the reaction of

[1] PUPIN, MICHAEL, "The New Reformation," page 118 *ff.*, Charles Scribner's Sons, 1927.

the flux in the air gap E breaks down and the air-gap becomes conductive. This releases the stored-up energy of the electrical flux, because the electrical charges on A and B move toward each other along the rods CD and the flux which is associated with them moves also. The energy of the electrical flux departs when the flux departs from the volume elements in which it was located; according to Maxwell's theory, it is transformed in every volume element of space into magnetic-flux energy. The disappearance of the electrical flux generates the magnetic flux, and it is a simple matter to form a picture of its location. In the immediate vicinity of the rods CD the curves of the magnetic flux must be interlinked with the rods and have a perfectly symmetrical distribution with respect to the axis of symmetry; that is, they are circular, the planes of the circles being perpendicular to this axis. At all other points of space they are also symmetrically distributed, and at each point in space the curves of the magnetic flux must be perpendicular to the curves of the electrical flux. At every point in space there is, according to Maxwell, a transmission of flux energy in the direction which is perpendicular to the direction of the electrical and of the magnetic flux. This transmission of energy is "electrical radiation." Hertz demonstrated experimentally the existence of this radiation; radio broadcasting is the offspring of this demonstration.

How did Hertz demonstrate the existence of electrical radiation which Maxwell's theory predicted? The answer is simple. If this radiation exists and follows the laws of the propagation of light, then in its passages from air to a dense material body it will be reflected. Hertz found that it was partially reflected by the walls of his laboratory, and in order to make the reflection more complete he placed a conducting screen in the path of the electrical radiation. Conductors, according to Maxwell's theory are opaque to electrical radiation, which is produced by rapidly varying electrical and magnetic fluxes, such as Hertz employed. His Leyden jar, the Hertzian oscillator, was so designed that, according to Thomson's calculation, mentioned above, its discharge was a vibratory one, having a frequency, a pitch, of many million vibrations per second. The waves of electrical and of magnetic flux actions radiated by the Hertzian oscillator were, therefore, oscillatory, and when reflected by the metal screen the incoming waves and the reflected waves should form by interference standing waves; that is to say, according to Maxwell there should be in the path of the electrical radiation maxima and minima of the electrical and of the magnetic flux action . . .

A READING BUDGET

For at least three or four months try to read on a schedule.

Beware of making this schedule too severe. Better an easy schedule at which you can succeed than an over-ambitious one at which you are bound to fail.

Begin with seven hours a week, distributing the time in any manner that fits in well with your other affairs. There isn't one business man in ten thousand who cannot, by careful planning, find this brief time for serious reading.

PART VI

PROGRESS CHART OF READING

As soon as you begin to study this book, start entries in this chart.

Make at least fifty entries on as many days. It is best not to make them on successive days, inasmuch as you will not improve your reading day by day, but rather in a series of spurts at irregular intervals.

It would be best if you could manage to make an entry every second or third day for the first two months, and perhaps once every five days during the third and fourth months.

As units of measure, select:

1. The first right-hand column of the first page of your favorite newspaper.

2. The first 1,000 words of the leading article in your favorite business periodical or technical journal.

3. The first 2,000 words of any heavy business reading which you have to cover regularly in the course of your day's work.

Date	Reading time for		
	1. Newspaper	2. Magazine	3. Business matter

Date	Reading time for		
	1. Newspaper	2. Magazine	3. Business matter

INDEX

A

Action habits and reading, 33
Adults, importance of reading of, 2
Air, and reading, 43
    results of bad, 43
Art of communication, 1
Average reading, exercises in, 204
    word rate in, 9

B

Body, momentary conditions of,
    and reading, 51
Books, number of, to be read in
    year, 10
Browsing, office-hour, 58
Budget, reading, 227
Business, and related reading
    matter, 59
    interests and reading, 59
    men, inaccuracies in reading of,
    55
    reading, when to do, 58

C

Communication, art of, 1
Comprehension, span of, 105
Conditions, momentary, of body,
    effect of on reading, 51
Content skimming, 35

D

Daydreaming, cause of poor reading,
    42

E

Easy reading, 39
Education, quintessence of, 13
Exercises in average reading, 204
    heavy reading, 225
    value of, in reading, 8
Eye grasp, how to improve, 86
    perception, how to test, 41
    reader, 54
    skimming, 35
    troubles, 26

F

Facts, main, reading for, 16, 17
Fatigue, muscular, 51

G

Grasp, eye, how to improve, 86
    how to estimate your, 105

H

Habits, action, 33
    and reading, 33
    reading, 23
    word, 22
    how to improve, 61
Heavy reading, exercises in, 225
    speed in, 10
Hoover, Herbert, 3
Hunger, effect of, on reading, 51, 52

I

Illumination, 27, 44
Improvement of reading, 37
Interest, kind of, determines method
    of reading, 19

231

CPSIA information can be obtained at www.ICGtesting.com
Printed in the USA
BVOW09s1547091214

378628BV00021B/315/P